The Stoic Father - Parenting from a Stoic Perspective Vol. 1

Phillip Deam

The Stoic Father - Parenting from a Stoic Perspective Vol. 1

CONTENTS

	Introduction	1
one	Parenting from a Place of Inner Calm	3
two	What We Can Control and What We Can't	37
three	Leading by Example	75
four	Patience Is Power	109
five	Raising Emotionally Resilient Children	146
six	The Gift of the Present Moment	183
	CONCLUSION	218

Copyright © 2025 by Phillip Deam
All rights reserved. No part of this book may be reproduced in any manner whatsoever without written permission except in the case of brief quotations embodied in critical articles and reviews.
First Printing, 2025

Introduction

My name is Phillip Deam, though, on social media i am "the philosophical dad"—a title that captures both my passion for age-old wisdom and my daily reality of being a hands-on father. I'm genuinely excited to share this book with you, because it represents more than just a collection of ideas: it's a window into my life as a husband, a dad, and a thinker who found a guiding light in Stoicism.

I'm blessed with a wonderful wife and three children who are the heartbeat of my world. My eldest son is six years old, navigating the unique challenges of sensory processing disorder with limited verbal skills. Supporting him can be equal parts miraculous and exhausting, as every new day demands patience, creativity, and emotional strength. My other children, too, fill our home with equal measures of joy and chaos. In all of this, my wife stands beside me as my rock—together, we've built a family dynamic that's both tested and enriched by our son's needs.

Discovering Stoicism was like finding a steady hand amid the whirlwinds of fatherhood. Early on, I recognized that calm and clarity—the cornerstones of Stoic philosophy—were exactly what I needed to shape a peaceful environment, not only for my son with special needs but for our entire household. I began to see how principles like self-control, acceptance, and mindful presence could anchor me in moments of chaos. Where once I might've felt overwhelmed by tantrums or unexpected meltdowns, Stoicism offered a blueprint for maintaining composure and leading with empathy.

In time, the wisdom of the Stoics became my compass. It granted me a renewed sense of direction, helping me keep sight of what truly matters: the emotional well-being of my children, the support of my wife, and my own inner balance. By practicing these ancient principles—flexibly, imperfectly, yet always with intention—I found fresh ways to connect with my son, empower my other kids, and grow as a person. It's incredible to watch each family member blossom when we weave these insights into our daily routines.

I'm sharing these lessons because I believe they can offer relief and inspiration to anyone willing to listen. Whether you're a parent facing similar challenges, an avid reader of philosophy, or simply someone curious about new strategies for staying centered, I hope you find a spark of insight in these pages. Stoicism has been an incredible gift in my life, and it's my sincerest hope that it becomes, in some way, a gift in yours as well.

One

Parenting from a Place of Inner Calm

"You have power over your mind—not outside events. Realize this, and you will find strength."
— Marcus Aurelius

Marcus Aurelius, one of the most prominent Stoic philosophers and the ruler of the Roman Empire, penned these words in his personal meditations. Despite juggling immense responsibilities and political turmoil, he steadfastly maintained that true power lies within the realm of our own minds. His assertion encourages us to focus on controlling our perceptions, judgments, and emotional reactions, rather than attempting to bend external events to our will.

From a broader Stoic and philosophical perspective, this quote captures a central tenet: while external circumstances—be they social, financial, or even global—are largely beyond our immediate influence, our internal world remains within our grasp. Modern psychological research echoes this sentiment in concepts like "cognitive reframing," where recognizing and reshaping negative thought patterns can significantly reduce stress and anxiety. By shifting our mindset, we move closer to what Dr. Jordan

Peterson might call "order," as opposed to the "chaos" of external unpredictability.

When applied to parenting, the implications become profound. Raising children involves countless unpredictable scenarios—tantrums, sibling rivalries, societal pressures—and it's easy to feel overwhelmed. Yet, by acknowledging that our power lies in our reactions rather than the events themselves, we can offer our children a stable, reassuring presence. Our calm responses set a powerful example, demonstrating how self-control fosters resilience and emotional well-being in the face of daily challenges.

Understanding Calm as a Parent
The Importance of Self-Mastery

Self-mastery is the bedrock of Stoic practice—a timeless guiding principle that compels us to cultivate virtues like patience, courage, and wisdom. As a 40-year-old father learning daily how to navigate the wild ride of parenthood, I have found that these virtues aren't just buzzwords but daily habits. When I consciously work on my own discipline and emotional control, I become a better role model for my kids. Stoic philosophy emphasizes that genuine power lies within our ability to govern ourselves. Marcus Aurelius once wrote, "You have power over your mind—not outside events. Realize this, and you will find strength." It underscores the importance of focusing on what we can truly shape: our thoughts, our actions, and our reactions. We sometimes forget how perceptive children are. They pick up on more than just our words; they sense our tensions, frustrations, and anxieties. By practicing calmness—whether through meditative moments before starting the day or nightly journal sessions—we gain the composure to handle everyday family chaos with a steadier heart.

When we exhibit poise under pressure, our children, almost unconsciously, begin to mirror that steadiness. It is a powerful reflection of how our inner state sets the emotional tone for our entire household. Over time, consistent calm leadership fosters a sense of security and trust within the family. Our kids learn they have a safe harbor in us, no matter how turbulent life's storms may get. For me, self-discipline has evolved into a continuous self-improvement project—one that pays dividends not just in my parenting but in every aspect of my life. When my children see me actively refining my own behavior—whether it is taking a deep breath during conflict, apologizing when I slip up, or persistently working toward better habits—they absorb the same skills for themselves. They learn that managing one's emotions is not an impossible feat but a daily practice. This quiet example teaches them to handle their own internal battles with resilience, ensuring they grow up equipped to face the world's challenges with grace and stability.

The Impact of a Centered Mindset on Family Life

Just like a thermostat quietly regulates the climate in our homes, our emotional state as parents sets the tone for everyone under our roof. I've noticed that when my stress levels spike—whether from a tight work deadline or the daily juggling of family obligations—my kids mirror that tension in their own ways. Stoicism reminds us that while we can't always prevent life from throwing us into a frenzy, we can manage how we respond. When we take a moment to breathe and pause before reacting, we help ensure that the entire household is less likely to boil over with conflict. This self-regulation doesn't just benefit us; it radiates outward, influencing the emotional climate for the whole family. When our internal pressures go unchecked, we risk succumbing to short tempers and reactive discipline. Whether it's yelling over a misplaced toy or overreacting to a sibling spat, the fallout can strain the parent-child bond and chip away at our own sense of composure. As Epictetus once taught, "It is not things themselves that disturb us, but our judgments about these things." By recognizing that our stress often stems from how we interpret and judge life's hurdles, we empower ourselves to shift our mindset. This shift can mean the difference between turning every minor challenge into a crisis and calmly guiding our children through everyday issues. Over time, creating a calm, stable environment at home pays immense dividends for our children's emotional well-being. Kids who grow up watching parents regulate their own stress learn valuable lessons about conflict resolution, empathy, and long-term thinking. When we're centered, we stop fixating on momentary aggravations and instead focus on the bigger picture—raising compassionate, resilient individuals who understand that difficulties are part of life, not the end of the world. Our steady presence becomes the blueprint for how they'll handle their own frustrations and relationships, setting them up for a future built on understanding, patience, and emotional health.

Philosophical Consistency: More Than an Ideal

Stoicism is not just a philosophy to ponder during quiet moments; it is a lifestyle that demands we act in alignment with our declared values. As a father aiming to weave Stoicism into everyday family life, I've realized that simply advising our children to "stay calm" or "be patient" falls short. Like any discipline, the real measure comes from our actions. Children are astute observers who quickly notice the gap between our words and our behaviors. If we profess to value patience but lose our temper over trivial matters, our actions will resonate more strongly with them than our words. In the Stoic tradition, there is a strong focus on embodying the virtues we advocate. Epictetus famously noted, "Don't explain your philosophy. Embody it." This is particularly relevant in parenting. By consistently demonstrating self-control, empathy, and courage in daily situations—whether it's dealing with a traffic jam calmly or addressing a neighbor's concerns with kindness—we teach our children how to face challenges. Each authentic display of composure enhances our credibility, making our children more open to our teachings about these same values. Crucially, aligning our actions with our words strengthens the bond between parent and child through mutual respect. When children observe that we genuinely live by the principles we promote, it fosters trust and admiration. It conveys to them, "My parent truly believes in this—enough to practice it even when faced with difficulties." Over time, these consistent expressions of virtue cultivate a home built on integrity and authenticity, demonstrating to our children a way of life grounded in true character and ethical behavior rather than mere slogans.

Laying the Groundwork for Growth

Calmness doesn't magically erase the inevitable ups and downs of family life, but it does grant us the clarity to tackle those challenges effectively. I've found that when I manage to keep my cool—even in the face of an unexpected meltdown or sibling rivalry—my children feel more secure. The absence of frantic energy in the room invites them to share their thoughts and feelings without fear of a harsh reaction. As the Stoic philosopher Seneca once said, "A gem cannot be polished without friction, nor a man perfected without trials." In other words, trials are a natural part of growth, and our calm demeanor helps ensure we're polishing rather than damaging our children's spirits along the way. When parents approach conflicts with thoughtful deliberation, children learn that their voices matter.

A stable emotional environment—one free from the storms of sudden anger or unchecked frustration—becomes fertile ground where curiosity thrives and resilience takes root. Kids begin to see that hardships and disagreements aren't catastrophes; they're opportunities to pause and say, "What can we learn here?" This mindset shift can transform household hiccups into teaching moments. Each time we handle a setback with poise, we model for our kids that obstacles can be met with patience and even a touch of creativity, rather than dread and panic. Calm parenting is, in many ways, the bedrock of trust, empathy, and moral development.

By viewing life's hardships as exercises in self-mastery, we show our children that virtues like patience and courage aren't just philosophical ideals—they're living tools we use daily. This approach not only fosters a sense of security and open communication, but it also establishes a moral compass that children can carry forward. They see firsthand that adversity can be an invitation to grow, and they learn to cherish the process of becoming better, kinder, and more resilient individuals.

Event vs. Interpretation

Self-mastery is the backbone of any Stoic practice—it's the daily, conscious effort to cultivate virtues like patience, courage, and wisdom. These qualities aren't meant for lofty discussions alone but are meant to be lived out in the everyday hustle and bustle of family life. For me as a father, this means pausing before reacting to that inevitable morning tantrum, reminding myself that true power lies in how I choose to respond. "Between stimulus and response, there is a space. In that space is our power to choose our response. In our response lies our growth and our freedom." - Viktor Frankl

One powerful aspect of self-mastery is understanding just how deeply attuned our children are to our emotions and behaviors. Kids are remarkably like sponges, absorbing every bit of our mood and energy, often without us even realizing it. If they sense our anger starting to bubble up, they will likely react with their own agitation and distress, mirroring the tension in the environment. Conversely, when we maintain an even keel—thanks to consistent mindfulness practices like journaling or meditation—our children pick up on that calmness and learn to reflect it back.

Over time, as they observe us routinely checking in with ourselves before allowing stress to dictate our responses, they begin to adopt similar practices themselves. This steady and reassuring presence creates a household environment that feels secure and nurturing rather than explosive, establishing a place where feelings can be expressed openly and safely, without the fear of irrational outbursts disrupting the harmony we strive to maintain. By practicing consistent, calm leadership, we not only create a haven of trust for our families but also offer our children a living blueprint for emotional management. When they observe us navigate life's turbulence with measured composure, it teaches them that self-discipline isn't about suppressing emotions, but about channeling them productively. In essence, self-mastery becomes a direct lesson in resilience. It shows our kids that the most effective way to handle adversity is not by fighting against every harsh wind, but by learning to remain steady within the storm. This example, lived out day by day, enriches their capacity for empathy, patience, and long-term well-being—one of the greatest gifts we can pass on as parents.

Mindset Shifts for Everyday Challenges

Every parent has faced moments when spilled milk at breakfast or an unexpected late-night school project seems to turn the household upside down. I'll admit, there have been times when such mishaps drove me straight to frustration, especially when juggling work deadlines or that elusive first cup of coffee. But in Stoic philosophy, moments like these are not merely inconveniences; they're opportunities to practice patience and problem-solving. As Epictetus reminds us, "It's not what happens to you, but how you react to it that matters." When we treat small crises as lessons rather than catastrophes, we show our children that life's bumps can be handled with steady composure.

Reframing these mishaps as growth opportunities doesn't mean pretending they're not inconvenient or time-consuming. Spilled milk still needs to be cleaned, and that last-minute school project still requires a flurry of late-night creativity. However, the essential shift is in our mindset. Instead of allowing annoyance to dictate our response, we can choose to guide our children through finding practical solutions—like delegating cleanup tasks or brainstorming project ideas together. This approach not only teaches kids how to tackle problems but also instills in them the idea that mistakes are part of learning, not grounds for panic or blame. When we consistently reframe challenges, we reduce those knee-jerk reactions that can escalate tension and damage trust.

Over time, our children watch and learn, developing their own calmer stance toward life's slip-ups. They absorb the lesson that while we can't always control what happens (be it a mess or a missed deadline), we can control our reactions. This nurturing of emotional resilience helps them build empathy toward themselves and others—an invaluable trait in a world full of unexpected twists and turns. By modeling a balanced response, we turn daily hassles into stepping stones for our kids' emotional maturity and our own personal growth as parents.

Cognitive Distortions to Watch For

It's surprising how often our minds jump to worst-case scenarios, especially in the midst of parenting. Perhaps your child forgets a homework assignment, and suddenly you're convinced they're on the path to perpetual underachievement. This tendency—known as catastrophizing—can escalate a small oversight into a colossal failure in our eyes. Stoicism teaches that we should focus on what we can truly control: our responses, not external circumstances. Marcus Aurelius once said, "You have power over your mind—not outside events.

Realize this, and you will find strength." When we reject the notion that one misstep is the end of the world, we guide our children with calm assurance rather than fear or alarm. In a similar vein, overgeneralizing ("This child never listens!") and personalization ("If my kid struggles, it's all my fault!") can erode our sense of balance. We lump together isolated incidents or hold ourselves solely responsible for every hiccup. The truth is, each child is a work in progress—just like we are—and we can't take credit or blame for every outcome. By keeping perspective, we foster a more accurate, compassionate view of our child's development and our role in it. This helps us avoid the shame or guilt that arises when we internalize their behavior as a direct reflection of our worth as parents.

We all experience moments when frustration clouds our judgment. In heated situations, it's easy to generalize: a child forgets their chores for the third time this week, leading us to think, "They never listen!" However, when we take a step back and consider what our children are going through, we see that one challenging moment doesn't define their overall behavior. Stoicism teaches us that maintaining a clear perspective allows for wise responses. As Seneca noted, "We suffer more often in imagination than in reality." When we let a single mistake or tough episode influence our entire view of our child, we suffer in our thoughts, jumping to conclusions that can strain our relationship. Similarly, personalization can weigh heavily on our hearts. When a child faces difficulties—be it academically or socially—we may feel it reflects our parenting: "I must have failed them." While our influence is significant, children are individual beings with their own personalities, experiences, and struggles.

Taking all the blame not only overlooks the child's own agency but also oversimplifies the intricate factors that influence their behavior and development. Kahlil Gibran wisely stated, "Your children are not your children. They are the sons and daughters of Life's longing for itself." This insight calls us to move beyond blame and towards support, acknowledging that our children have their own unique paths to navigate. By focusing on how we can assist them, rather than being mired in guilt or shame, we create a more nurturing family environment. We must release the unrealistic expectation of being perfect disciplinarians or flawless guides and instead fully embrace our role as dedicated partners in our children's learning journeys.

This compassionate viewpoint allows us to respond with empathy when our kids falter, reinforcing the idea that mistakes are part of the learning process, not indicators of failure. It also teaches self-forgiveness, demonstrating to children that making mistakes and learning from them is integral to growth. When we replace overgeneralization with understanding and personalization with balanced accountability, we create a healthier environment for everyone in the family to grow with grace and resilienceThen come those tricky "should" statements: "They should know better by now!" or "I should be doing more!" Such rigid expectations set us up for disappointment and resentment.

Instead, we can replace these distortions with balanced, reality-based thinking that acknowledges both our children's and our own ongoing growth. We're all learning—spilling milk one day, conquering new challenges the next. By recognizing and gently correcting these cognitive pitfalls, we cultivate a healthier environment where communication thrives, problems are solved more effectively, and everyone (yes, even parents) is given the grace to evolve.

Tying Reframing to Stoic Practices

One of the powerful tools in Stoicism is the practice of imagining worst-case scenarios—a technique aimed not at dwelling on negativity, but at lessening the grip of anxiety on our daily lives. For parents, this might mean mentally rehearsing how we would respond if a family vacation gets derailed or if our child faces repeated bullying at school. By acknowledging that unexpected challenges can and will occur, we are better prepared to meet them with level-headed composure. As the Stoics often reminded us, "We suffer more in imagination than in reality," and if we allow ourselves a brief, controlled space to consider potential obstacles, we develop a resilience that can cushion the blow when real trials arise.

A key Stoic principle that supports this mindset is "amor fati," which translates to "love of fate." Rather than viewing hardships as merely unfortunate events, amor fati encourages us to see them as integral parts of life's tapestry—and essential stepping stones to growth. For parents, adopting this perspective can transform a child's sudden academic setback or a messy sibling feud from a dreaded inconvenience into an opportunity for deeper connection and teaching. When our kids see us approach adversity not with panic or frustration but with calm acceptance and thoughtful guidance, they learn firsthand what resilience looks like in action.

This process helps them develop the emotional muscle memory they will need to navigate their own setbacks as they grow. What is most striking is how seamlessly this philosophical stance aligns with modern concepts of psychological resilience. By reframing events through a Stoic lens—anticipating that life comes with its share of bumps and twists—parents reduce their chronic stress and model healthier responses for the entire household. Disagreements and disappointments become less about winning and more about learning. In the grand scheme, this fortifies family bonds because children sense that Mom or Dad isn't perpetually rattled by life's curveballs. Over time, the household dynamic shifts: resilience becomes an ingrained value, helping everyone move through life's inevitable storms with greater emotional stability and shared understanding.

Practical Reframing Techniques

It's one thing to know we should stay calm; it's another thing entirely to do so when emotions run high. That's why it's helpful to have a few concrete techniques at the ready. One of my personal favorites is "Pause and Label." In the midst of a meltdown or a heated argument, instead of blurting out the first frustrated thought that comes to mind, I take a moment—sometimes just a single breath—and label the emotion I'm experiencing: anger, impatience, or fear. This momentary pause reminds me that these feelings are fleeting signals, not permanent truths. Motivational speaker Brian Tracy said that "You cannot control what happens to you, but you can control your attitude toward what happens to you." Recognizing that power starts with naming what's brewing inside. The next step is asking ourselves, "What Can I Control?"

In parenting, it's easy to slip into the mentality that we must control our children's every action or outcome. But the reality, as any parent of a spirited child knows, is that we have far more influence over our own mindset, tone, and consistency than we do over someone else's behavior. When kids see that we focus on how we respond—rather than on manipulating their choices—they feel more respected and become more open to problem-solving. That's where "Seek Solutions Together" comes in. Involving children in brainstorming not only helps diffuse tension but also empowers them. They see themselves as active participants in resolving family issues, rather than passive recipients of discipline or blame.

Simple habits like Reflecting in Writing and Celebrating Small Wins can help anchor these reframing techniques in our daily lives. Even jotting down a few thoughts in a journal can transform chaos into clarity, capturing the lessons hidden in each challenge. Acknowledging small victories—whether it's your child calmly putting away toys or you catching yourself before snapping—reinforces a positive outlook. Over time, these practices build an environment of trust and open communication. Everyone in the family learns that mistakes and missteps aren't disasters; they're opportunities for growth, improved understanding, and genuine connection.

Emotional Regulation and Leading by Example

Many people confuse the concept of Stoic detachment with shutting down emotions altogether, but there is a world of difference between recognizing your feelings and ignoring them. True Stoic detachment means observing emotions—both yours and your child's—without allowing them to completely take control. It is about understanding that frustration, disappointment, or even anger are part of the human experience. These emotions are not the problem; it is what we do with them that makes or breaks our relationships.

As Marcus Aurelius wrote, "The happiness of your life depends upon the quality of your thoughts." When we recognize a surge of frustration and consciously decide how to respond, we practice genuine detachment: we see the emotion clearly, but we do not let it dictate our behavior. Emotional suppression, on the other hand, is like putting a lid on a boiling pot and hoping it never spills over. Sooner or later, the pressure becomes too great, leading to explosive outbursts or simmering resentment. As parents, it is crucial to show our children that emotions can be acknowledged and released in healthy ways. When we stuff them down or pretend everything is fine—especially if our facial expressions and body language suggest otherwise—our kids pick up on the disconnect. In the long term, this can create confusion and distrust, as children may feel something is "off" even if we insist we are okay.

That is why the balanced approach involves embracing emotions as signals while keeping a clear head about what action to take next. By calmly reflecting on what we are feeling and why, we teach our children the art of emotional intelligence. For example, telling your child, "Dad is feeling frustrated right now because the day did not go as planned, but let's figure out a solution together," models authentic communication.

Kids learn that emotions do not need to be hidden or feared—they can be navigated with honesty and empathy. In doing so, we build a family culture where feelings are acknowledged, but never used as weapons or allowed to run rampant. This approach lays the groundwork for healthier conflict resolution, stronger bonds, and a more resilient mindset in both parents and children alike.

Why Parental Composure Matters

When children look at us—whether we're aware of it in the moment or not—they take their emotional cues from how we react. If we respond to spilled juice on the couch or a noisy sibling spat with frantic energy, we effectively teach them that crisis mode is the default setting for handling conflict. Conversely, when we consistently exhibit calmness—even in the face of unexpected frustrations—we show our children a more measured way to cope. They learn to pause, breathe, and consider their options rather than lashing out with anger or despair.

A composed parent also tends to de-escalate problems before they morph into shouting matches or slamming doors. When we keep our heads level, we slow down the pace of conflict, transforming stressful moments into teachable ones. Composure doesn't mean we never feel annoyance or disappointment—it simply means we've learned to recognize those feelings and respond in ways that foster solutions instead of more chaos. As Seneca wrote, "No man is free who is not master of himself." By modeling self-mastery under pressure, we demonstrate to our children that confidence stems not from dominating others but from guiding ourselves with clear thought and steady presence.

Moreover, children flourish in predictable environments where they can trust that a parent's reaction won't swing wildly from day to day. When we keep our emotional state consistent, we're more likely to make fair, thoughtful disciplinary decisions. This reliability helps our kids feel safe and grounded, reinforcing the core bond of trust in our relationship. Over time, it cultivates emotional security and allows children to develop resilience. They learn that life will have its rough patches, but that calmness and clear thinking can transform even the stormiest circumstances into opportunities for growth—and that's a lesson they'll carry with them well beyond childhood.

Recognizing and Managing Triggers

We all have those moments when something—a roll of the eyes, a sibling squabble, or a defiant tone—lights a fuse inside us. These triggers can catch us off guard and transform our usual calm into frustration in the blink of an eye. Stoic philosophy reminds us that our power lies not in controlling external events but in managing our internal responses. When we identify the specific behaviors or situations that set us off, we give ourselves a chance to prepare for them. Think of it like a practice drill: we can't stop the "fire" of a trigger from occurring, but with awareness, we can learn where the exits are and how to prevent the flame from spreading. The first step is self-awareness. Often, our body signals a brewing storm before our mind even registers it.

A clenching jaw, racing thoughts, or a spike in irritability can be our early warning system. By paying attention to these cues—maybe even jotting them down in a journal—we begin to notice patterns: certain times of day, certain words, certain tones of voice. Once we have that awareness, we can deploy techniques to interrupt the stress cycle. It might be as simple as taking a deep breath, stepping away for a quick walk, or mentally reframing the situation. In those precious few seconds, we shift from reacting on impulse to responding with intention. Over time, practicing these strategies not only calms the immediate storm but also rewires how we handle difficult moments.

We gradually train ourselves to rely on measured wisdom instead of reflexive anger. Children, in turn, learn by watching us. When they see a parent pause, breathe, and respond thoughtfully, it speaks louder than any lecture on "keeping cool." It shows them a real-world blueprint for managing big emotions—an invaluable skill that will serve them in school, friendships, and beyond. By recognizing our triggers and taking steps to manage them, we model the art of self-mastery, building a stronger, more trusting parent-child bond in the process.

Drawing from Peterson and Holiday

Jordan Peterson often reminds us that before we can bring order to our families, we need to tame the chaos within ourselves. In his view, establishing stable routines, setting clear moral guidelines, and taking responsibility for our actions create a ripple effect throughout the household. I've seen this firsthand in my own family life: when I let my sleep schedule, stress management, or work commitments become disorganized, the kids inevitably feel the tremors of my unrest. A solid routine—whether it's regular family mealtime or consistent bedtime rituals—can act as the scaffolding that supports a calmer, more harmonious environment.

Ryan Holiday, on the other hand, brings Stoicism into the modern sphere, showing how obstacles can be transformed into opportunities for growth. This isn't just about turning professional setbacks or financial strain into wisdom; it applies to our parenting hurdles as well. Each time our child acts out, or our patience is tested by the tenth "but why?" question in a single hour, we can choose to see these moments as stepping stones. They become chances to practice virtues like patience and empathy, rather than inconveniences to overcome. Holiday's work reminds us that real progress often comes through adversity—when we learn to face challenges with grace, we set the stage for deeper family bonds and stronger moral character.

Both Peterson and Holiday underscore the importance of personal responsibility: real change doesn't start from "out there" in the world, but rather from within our own minds and daily actions. Our composure in tough moments isn't just about performing calmness for the sake of appearance; it's a reflection of our inner discipline and our commitment to living by our highest values. By integrating these insights into daily life—taking charge of our own chaos and reframing setbacks as growth opportunities—we merge philosophical ideals with real-world practicality. Our children learn not only from what we say but from how we embody these principles, witnessing a father who chooses to lead with composure, authenticity, and unwavering love.

Cultivating Emotional Safety

The Story of the Oak and the Reeds

In Aesop's fable, a proud and sturdy **oak** tree mocks the slender **reeds** growing nearby. The oak believes its massive trunk and roots make it far superior to the flimsy reeds that bend with every breeze. However, a powerful storm arrives and unleashes fierce winds, uprooting the unyielding oak. Meanwhile, the reeds survive by bending with the gusts and then straightening once it's calm.

Parenting is undeniably a tumultuous journey, filled with tantrums, unexpected changes, and societal pressures that can easily disrupt our peace if we cling too tightly to our expectations. Embracing stoic acceptance empowers us to recognize that while we cannot control external events, we can master our internal adaptability—much like reeds that bend gracefully in the wind. By concentrating on what we can influence—our responses, our tone of voice, our willingness to adjust—we instill in our children the invaluable lesson that calm resilience is far superior to stubborn resistance. By practicing emotional flexibility, we not only prevent ourselves from breaking under stress but also create a nurturing environment. We demonstrate to our kids that even in the face of life's storms, a steady parent who bends rather than breaks can navigate any challenge with grace and strength.

One of the most impactful gifts we can offer our children is the sense that it's safe to bring us their fears, missteps, and confusions. When I first became a dad, I naively thought "holding it together" simply meant not yelling. But over time, I've discovered there's a deeper layer: a calm and open presence that invites our kids to confide in us without fear of shame or punishment. Stoicism teaches that genuine strength isn't about towering over others or never showing emotion—it's about exercising self-control and empathy, ensuring those around us feel acknowledged and protected. When we can respond calmly, we open a door for our children to share what's truly on their minds. Through this open dialogue, our children gain something incredibly valuable: emotional literacy. It's not just about them knowing how they feel—though that's a big part of it—but about learning to put those feelings into words. By encouraging them to say, "I'm frustrated because my project didn't go as planned," or, "I'm worried I won't make any friends this year," we help them develop a vocabulary for life's inner challenges. As Epictetus advised, "We cannot always choose our external circumstances, but we can choose how we respond." Helping children identify and articulate their feelings teaches them that emotions, while sometimes intense, can be understood and managed constructively. Perhaps most importantly, a calm parental response sets the tone for how problems are addressed as a team. Instead of erupting into outbursts—which often push kids to withdraw or hide their mistakes—our steady demeanor reassures them we're on their side. In this environment, children's self-esteem grows because they feel genuinely accepted, even when they stumble. They see that conflict and errors aren't deal-breakers, but stepping stones to learning. This sense of safety propels them toward becoming self-reliant, empathetic individuals who approach life's challenges with courage, knowing they can count on support—and a listening ear—whenever they need it.

The Mindful Pause
Why Pausing is Powerful

Have you ever felt that surge of frustration—like a sudden lightning bolt—when your child repeatedly ignores your instructions, or when a sibling fight erupts just as you're rushing out the door? In those moments, our instinct can be to snap back, often regretting our words seconds later. That's where the simple but profound act of pausing comes in. As the Stoics taught, wisdom begins with the awareness of our initial impulses. A brief pause before we speak or act can transform knee-jerk reactions into thoughtful responses. Seneca once said, "It does not matter what you bear, but how you bear it," reminding us that a mere few seconds of self-restraint can shift the entire emotional tone of a confrontation. When we intentionally pause, we're applying a core Stoic principle: measured speech and action. Emotions can flare up in a heartbeat, but they also cool down more quickly when given space. This moment of stillness allows us to acknowledge our anger or frustration without letting it take the driver's seat. Instead of flying off the handle, we step back and ask ourselves: "What's really going on here? How can I address this in a way that aligns with my values?" By doing so, we prevent ourselves from blurting out harsh words or doling out punishments we'll later regret. This deliberate shift fosters an atmosphere of understanding rather than tension. Kids are surprisingly observant of how we handle conflicts. When they see us pause—perhaps taking a breath or quietly collecting our thoughts—they learn that big emotions don't have to dictate our behavior. This microcosm of self-control, played out in everyday moments, lays the groundwork for how they'll handle their own frustrations in life. They see that the pause isn't just empty silence; it's a powerful tool for re-calibration and reflection. Over time, they begin to mirror that composure, turning what might have been wild arguments into more constructive, empathetic conversations. By valuing the pause, we pass on a vital lesson: we are never slaves to our emotions; we can always choose how we respond.

Techniques for Implementing the Pause

Sometimes, the simplest techniques can make the biggest difference. One go-to method is to count to three—either counting silently in your head or taking three slow, intentional breaths before speaking. This brief interval allows the initial wave of frustration or panic to subside, giving you that crucial window to choose your words more carefully. It might feel a bit forced at first, especially when tensions are running high, but think of it as a small investment that pays off in a calmer, more constructive interaction. As the Stoics remind us, a moment's delay can prevent a chain reaction of heated emotions. Another powerful approach involves a physical reset. Sometimes, all it takes to break the tension is to stand up from your seat, stretch your arms, or take a quick sip of water. These seemingly trivial actions interrupt the stress cycle, creating a pause long enough for the rational part of your brain to catch up. During this pause, engage in a brief inner dialogue, silently asking yourself, "What's the best way to handle this?" or "How can I stay aligned with my values right now?" This question-centered self-talk helps reorient your thoughts away from immediate annoyance and toward a more measured response, reflecting the Stoic principle of focusing on what you can control—your mindset. To keep these strategies front and center, consider using a visual cue like a wristband, a phone reminder, or even a sticky note on your fridge to prompt mindful pausing. This is especially helpful when you're forming the habit, as it keeps the idea of pausing in your peripheral awareness. And don't forget to practice in low-stakes situations—whether that's dealing with a minor spill or waiting in a slow grocery line. By building the pause habit during everyday annoyances, you'll be better prepared to maintain your composure during bigger parenting challenges. Over time, these small, deliberate pauses accumulate into a consistent pattern of thoughtful communication—an invaluable lesson in emotional regulation for both you and your children

Link to Cognitive Behavioral Techniques

Cognitive Behavioral Therapy (CBT) reminds us that there is a process between what happens to us (the stimulus) and how we ultimately respond (the action). It is that middle step—our thoughts and emotions—that determines whether we explode or calmly address a situation. Stoicism, centuries before modern psychology, offered a similar perspective: while we cannot always direct external circumstances, we can train ourselves to manage our internal judgments. Michel de Montaigne famously observed, "My life has been full of terrible misfortunes—most of which never happened," emphasizing how our minds can distort reality more than reality itself demands. This insight resonates with CBT's focus on redirecting unhelpful thought patterns. One powerful technique shared by both traditions is the pause, visualized as the "thought → feeling → action" chain: by inserting a deliberate moment of awareness, we gain space to choose a more constructive response.

If we can catch ourselves right after the thought, we have a chance to change the entire outcome. By slowing down the process, we can reframe the situation, choosing to respond with measured wisdom rather than reflexive anger. This skill does not just help us avoid regretful outbursts; it also teaches our children what healthy emotional regulation looks like.

When kids see us interrupt that chain of frustration—perhaps by taking a deep breath or stepping aside for a moment—they learn that feelings do not have to control actions. They, too, can pause, reflect, and steer the interaction onto a calmer path. Over time, integrating Stoic wisdom with CBT tools can significantly reduce stress throughout the whole family. When we make a habit of checking our automatic thoughts, we are less likely to snap at minor inconveniences or escalate small issues into major conflicts. Children, witnessing these calmer interactions, begin to adopt similar patterns for handling their own frustrations. The result is a household where emotional flare-ups diminish and understanding grows. In this sense, modern therapy and ancient philosophy become perfect partners, each strengthening the other's ability to promote mental clarity, resilience, and genuine connection among family members.

The Pause as a Teaching Moment

When tensions spike in the household—maybe it's a fight over screen time or a standoff about chores—it's all too tempting to snap out orders just to restore calm. But a well-timed pause can change everything, allowing us to shift from authoritarian to collaborative problem-solving. Instead of barking commands in the heat of anger, take that crucial moment to breathe and then calmly invite your child's perspective. "What do you think the fairest solution might be?" or "How would you handle this if you were me?" These simple questions do more than ease tensions; they signal respect and a willingness to listen, which often diffuses defiance and frustration on the spot. By involving children in the process, we're not ceding our authority as parents—far from it. Rather, we're teaching them critical thinking, empathy, and responsibility. They get to see firsthand that their viewpoint matters, and that conflicts aren't something to either run from or bulldoze through. This sense of shared ownership in problem-solving can turn a heated clash into a moment of genuine connection. In Stoic terms, we're guiding our children toward understanding that external events (like a disagreement) are less significant than how we choose to address them together. As Epictetus would say, "It's not what happens, but how we respond to what happens that counts." What's more, demonstrating calm dialogue under pressure isn't just a short-term fix—it lays the groundwork for healthier communication well into the future. When children see this approach repeated over time, they internalize the lesson that conflict doesn't have to be destructive; it can be a catalyst for growth and mutual respect. They learn that their parents aren't perfect robots devoid of emotion, but individuals dedicated to managing stress constructively and modeling the kind of discourse we'd all like to see in the world. It's an invaluable skill that, once learned at home, they'll carry into friendships, school settings, and eventually into their own adult relationships.

Consistency: The Hardest but Most Rewarding Part

The beauty—and the challenge—of the pause technique lies in its everyday application, especially on those days when fatigue and stress cloud our best intentions. Even with a deep commitment to self-mastery, there are moments when our well-practiced pause slips through our fingers. When we're running on empty or overwhelmed by the demands of work, home, and life, it's natural to have lapses. In these moments, the key is not to wallow in guilt but to recognize the slip-up as part of the process. After all, as the Stoics remind us, perfection is not the goal—growth is. Each missed opportunity provides us with invaluable feedback on our emotional state and serves as an invitation to return to mindful practice with renewed determination. Every time we successfully implement a pause, however small, it reinforces the habit and gently nudges it toward becoming second nature. Think of it as building a muscle: consistency, even in the face of setbacks, is what eventually makes the act of pausing almost automatic. Over time, as we learn to catch our initial impulses before they spiral, we transform stress into a space for reflection and calm. This transformation isn't instantaneous—it's cumulative, built day by day through practice and persistence. The process teaches us to be patient with ourselves, echoing Epictetus's wisdom that "No great thing is created suddenly," reminding us that mastery of our responses is a journey, not an overnight achievement. Children are perhaps the greatest beneficiaries of our perseverance. They watch us stumble and then courageously pick ourselves back up, learning a fundamental life lesson: mistakes are not failures but opportunities for growth. When they see us acknowledge a lapse, learn from it, and continue striving for consistent self-control, we help cultivate a resilient mindset in them. Over time, this consistency shapes a calmer, more harmonious household culture, where setbacks are seen not as flaws but as stepping stones toward better emotional regulation and deeper understanding. Ultimately, by embracing the challenge of daily practice, we demonstrate that true self-control is less about never faltering and more about continuously striving to be the best versions of ourselves.

Fostering Resilience in Children
Teaching by Living Example

When we strive for stoic calm in our daily lives, we offer our children a real-life blueprint for resilience and problem-solving. Children are exceptionally perceptive and learn a great deal from observing how we handle adversity. When they see us remain composed in the face of challenges—be it a hectic morning or an unexpected setback—they internalize the value of calm persistence. As Marcus Aurelius wisely noted, "If you are distressed by anything external, the pain is not due to the thing itself, but to your estimate of it; and this you have the power to revoke at any moment." In these moments, our actions speak louder than our words, teaching our children that challenges, no matter how daunting, can be met with clear-headed determination.

Moreover, demonstrating self-control during adversity isn't just about handling difficult moments; it's also about aligning our actions with our core values, thereby modeling integrity. When we live out our principles—whether it's treating others with respect during a heated discussion or acknowledging our mistakes gracefully—we show our children that virtue is not merely an abstract concept but a practical guide for everyday decisions. This kind of modeling offers them concrete examples of how to translate values into actions. The calm, authoritative presence we establish in our homes serves as a foundation for better guidance and discipline. It reassures our kids that although setbacks may occur, they can be managed with wisdom and compassion.

The story of St. George and the Dragon is a powerful narrative that embodies the themes of resilience and triumph over adversity. According to legend, St. George was a valiant knight who encountered a fearsome dragon that terrorized a town. The dragon demanded sacrifices from the townspeople, and in a desperate attempt to appease it, they offered their own children. When the king's daughter was chosen as the next sacrifice, the town was plunged into despair. St. George, upon hearing of the plight of the townspeople, resolved to confront the dragon. Armed only with his faith and courage, he rode out to meet the creature. The battle was fierce, and the dragon's ferocity was matched only by St. George's determination. Despite the overwhelming odds, St. George did not waver. He drew upon his inner strength, refusing to let fear paralyze him. With a final, valiant effort, St. George struck the dragon down, liberating the town from its terror. His victory was not merely over the dragon but also symbolized the triumph of hope and bravery in the face of insurmountable challenges. The townspeople rejoiced, and the king honored St. George as a hero. This story illustrates the essence of resilience—the capacity to endure and overcome hardships. St. George's journey reflects the idea that true strength lies in facing fears head-on, even when the situation seems dire. His unwavering spirit serves as a reminder that adversity can be confronted with courage, leading to personal growth and the empowerment of others. The tale encourages individuals to embrace their challenges, for it is through these trials that one can emerge stronger and more capable of triumphing over future obstacles.

Over time, as children witness and emulate these traits, they begin to mirror our stoic approach not just at home but also in their interactions with peers and in personal challenges. They learn that resilience is built on a consistent practice of thoughtful responses rather than reactive impulses. Such behavior fosters a sense of self-reliance and emotional maturity, equipping them to navigate both personal and social hurdles. As our children adopt these lessons, they develop a stronger sense of self, understanding that the true mark of strength lies in how calmly and effectively one can face life's inevitable storms. This lasting impact reaffirms that our best lessons are not those taught in words, but those demonstrated in every mindful, resilient action we take.

Balancing Support and Independence

Stoicism emphasizes the importance of emotional resilience while also maintaining strong connections with loved ones and family. It advocates for the provision of wise support that encourages individuals to navigate their own personal challenges effectively. This fundamental principle aligns seamlessly with the idea of fostering independence in children.

By allowing children to face age-appropriate challenges and struggles, parents can actively promote their confidence, self-reliance, and overall growth. This approach not only helps children develop essential life skills but also strengthens the bonds within families as they learn to support one another.

Encouraging independence in children involves offering guidance in a way that supports them without overwhelming them with excessive control. This thoughtful approach not only helps children develop essential problem-solving skills but also fosters a strong sense of trust in their own abilities. As they learn to navigate various difficulties, they do so with a growing sense of autonomy and confidence. While it is important for parents to step in when necessary to provide support, this intervention should always be purposeful and serve a teaching function. By doing so, parents equip their children with the valuable tools and understanding they need to manage similar situations independently in the future, ultimately helping them grow into capable and self-reliant individuals.

A balanced strategy that effectively merges support with independence helps avoid overprotectiveness, which can hinder personal growth and development. By encouraging a strong sense of responsibility, parents can significantly assist their children in building resilience and equipping them to tackle life's challenges independently. This approach ultimately prepares them for increased independence as they transition into adulthood. Such a mindful balance creates a nurturing atmosphere where emotional support and personal growth can thrive together, enabling children to flourish and become well-rounded individuals.

From Discipline to Self-Discipline

When we first introduce rules to our children, these boundaries often come from an external source—ourselves. However, over time, the goal is not just to impose discipline but to help our kids internalize self-discipline. In other words, external rules become meaningful only when they evolve into personal guidelines that the child chooses to follow. I have learned that a calm and consistent parenting style can transform seemingly arbitrary rules into fair, understandable principles that resonate on a deeper level. As the Stoics teach us, the true battle is not against the external world but within ourselves; by aligning our own actions with our core values, we encourage our children to mirror that behavior. A key part of this transformation lies in explaining the rationale behind the rules. When we take the time to articulate why a particular rule exists—whether it is for safety, respect, or mutual harmony—we provide our children with insight into its larger purpose. Instead of feeling like they are being controlled by unpredictable edicts, kids learn that these guidelines are rooted in thoughtfulness and shared values. This not only builds respect and cooperation but also reduces power struggles as they begin to understand and appreciate the principles guiding their behavior. In this light, discipline shifts from a top-down imposition to a collaborative effort in nurturing personal responsibility. Over the long run, these small shifts in perspective add up, paving the way for our children to adopt their own codes of conduct. Instead of merely obeying because they are told to, they learn to operate from a place of self-regulation—where discipline comes from within. This evolution from enforced discipline to self-discipline is one of the greatest gifts we can provide as parents. It equips our children with the resilience and integrity necessary for adulthood, forging a legacy of thoughtful, principled behavior that extends far beyond the walls of our home.

Emphasizing Growth over Perfection

In our modern world, perfectionism is often glorified, yet it can be a heavy burden on both parents and children. The pursuit of flawlessness tends to breed a fear of failure and a relentless stress that inhibits genuine learning. Stoic philosophy reminds us that mistakes are not the antithesis of success but a natural part of the human condition. As Marcus Aurelius taught, "The impediment to action advances action. What stands in the way becomes the way." This perspective encourages us to view setbacks as stepping stones—essential opportunities to learn and refine our approach to life, rather than as definitive marks of inadequacy. Encouraging children to see mistakes as lessons fosters an environment where growth is valued above a pristine record of success. When children witness that real effort, curiosity, and resilience are celebrated more than flawless results, they learn that being human means evolving through challenges. Explaining the Stoic idea of "amor fati"—the love of one's fate—can help them understand that every misstep is part of their unique journey. It is about embracing all experiences, both good and bad, as opportunities to improve. This philosophy not only alleviates the pressure to be perfect but also builds a foundation of self-compassion, where setbacks are simply cues to take another, wiser step forward. When children feel safe to make mistakes without judgment, they develop the confidence needed to take on new challenges. A home environment that values effort over perfection creates a haven where vulnerability transforms into strength. As parents, our role is to model this mindset: celebrating the learning process and encouraging perseverance even when the outcomes are less than perfect. Over time, this approach instills in our children a resilient spirit—a readiness to see every obstacle as a chance to grow, and every stumble as part of the dance of life. In doing so, we equip them with not just a set of skills, but a way of thinking that turns challenges into catalysts for lifelong personal development.

Creating a Legacy of Self-Reliance

A home governed by calm, principled leadership is more than just a pleasant environment; it is an incubator for future generations of resilient, self-reliant individuals. When children witness their parents handling challenges with measured thought and compassion, they internalize those behaviors as natural responses to adversity. It is like watching a master craftsman at work: every gesture, every pause before a reaction, every thoughtful decision becomes part of the child's repertoire. This continuous exposure to steady, reflective leadership is not simply about maintaining order in the present; it plants the seeds for a lifelong capacity for critical thinking, emotional regulation, and wise decision-making.

As our children grow up in a household where Stoic values are more than just words on a page, these principles seep into their character. They learn that self-reliance is not about going it alone in a cold world; it is about possessing the inner tools to navigate life's challenges without being overwhelmed by them. The virtues of courage, wisdom, and empathy—practiced daily through our responses to both minor frustrations and major setbacks—serve as the backbone of this inner toolkit. Over time, these emotional tools become so ingrained that they naturally guide our children's actions, whether in moments of personal disappointment or when mediating disputes among friends. They begin to see that the most potent form of discipline is self-discipline—a discipline born out of self-awareness and a genuine respect for the ups and downs of life.

This legacy of self-reliance extends beyond the individual family, gradually influencing communities and even future generations. When children learn to handle their emotions effectively and solve problems collaboratively, they carry those skills into school, friendships, and eventually the workplace. They become the calm voices in chaotic situations—people who can be trusted to lead with integrity because they understand that true leadership is anchored in self-control, not coercion. Parents who embody these principles create a ripple effect; their children, in turn, become role models to their peers, spreading the ethos of thoughtful, intentional living far beyond the confines of the home. Ultimately, parenting from a place of inner calm paves the way for a more harmonious society.

The legacy we create is not measured by material success, but by the enduring impact of the values we instill. When our children grow into self-reliant adults, they not only carry forward the lessons learned at home but also contribute to a larger culture where emotional resilience and principled action are prized assets. This transformation—from enforced order to a naturally emerging, internally motivated way of living—is the true hallmark of a legacy well-crafted. In the end, the seeds of calm, reflective leadership that we nurture in our homes can flourish into a lifetime of resilience, touching lives in ways we may never fully see but can be profoundly proud of.

Key Takeaways (Chapter Cheat Sheet)

1. Your Inner World Is Your Domain

    ◦ By focusing on what you can control—your mindset and reactions—you set a calmer tone for the entire family.
2. Reframing Builds Resilience

- Viewing challenges as opportunities to learn fosters patience, empathy, and problem-solving skills in both parent and child.
3. Model Calm Under Pressure

    - Children closely watch how you handle stress. Demonstrating composure teaches them self-regulation.
4. Use the Mindful Pause

    - Pausing before responding defuses tension and encourages more thoughtful communication.
5. Consistency Over Time

    - Applying Stoic principles daily, even in small ways, creates a family culture of emotional stability and personal growth.

Reflection Prompts

1. Journaling Exercise

    - Recall a recent parenting moment when you felt your emotions rising. How could a mindful pause or reframing have changed the outcome?
2. Family Discussion

    - Share with your child (in an age-appropriate way) a time you used calm thinking to solve a problem. Ask them if they've ever tried something similar.
3. Action Step

- Pick one "trigger" that typically provokes frustration and commit to practicing the mindful pause next time it arises. Keep a short log of the results.

Cultivating a calm inner mindset lays the foundation for a more peaceful and rewarding parenting journey. By focusing on what you can control—your perspective, emotions, and responses—you model resilience and wisdom for your children.

Two

What We Can Control and What We Can't

The chief task in life is simply this: to identify and separate matters so that I can say clearly to myself which are externals not under my control, and which have to do with the choices I actually control."
— *Epictetus*

Epictetus was a Greek Stoic philosopher whose teachings often revolved around the concept of personal agency. His life story is particularly compelling—born a slave, he rose to become one of the most influential moral teachers of his time. In this quote, Epictetus presents us with the foundation of Stoic philosophy: the dichotomy of control, or the clear distinction between what lies within our power and what does not.

From a philosophical angle, this principle encourages us to direct our efforts toward cultivating our character, judgments, and emotional responses rather than wasting energy on external events we can never fully influence. Modern psychology echoes this wisdom in areas like stress management and cognitive-behavioral therapy (CBT), where identifying controllable vs. uncontrollable factors helps reduce anxiety. By focusing on our inner choices, we free ourselves from the perpetual chase of trying to bend the outside world to our will.

For parents, the pressure to "do it all" can be overwhelming—managing schedules, shaping children's futures, and responding to social expectations all pile on. Yet, when we recognize that certain aspects of parenting (like a child's temperament or societal changes) are beyond our direct influence, we can shift our attention toward what truly matters: our own mindset, our habits of communication, and the way we model resilience. Letting go of the illusion of total control not only reduces stress, but also empowers us to become more thoughtful, present, and compassionate guides for our children.

The Dichotomy of Control in Parenting
Understanding What Is Truly Ours to Shape

The concept of The Dichotomy of Control in parenting emphasizes the distinction between what parents can influence and what lies beyond their control. In Stoicism, this idea is framed around recognizing that our judgments, intentions, and actions are truly ours to shape. In the context of parenting, this translates into the awareness that while parents can set a tone and model values, they cannot dictate a child's behavior or interests.

Focusing on what is truly ours to shape means that parents should concentrate on creating a nurturing environment where values such as respect, kindness, and resilience are demonstrated consistently. By modeling these values, parents can influence their children's development in meaningful ways, fostering an atmosphere that encourages children to adopt similar behaviors. Establishing clear boundaries is also crucial; it provides children with a sense of security and understanding of acceptable behaviors.

Attempting to control or force specific outcomes, such as a child's perfect behavior or alignment with parental interests, often leads to power struggles. These struggles can create tension and anxiety, both for the parent and the child. When parents exert pressure for specific results, it can lead to resistance and rebellion in children, ultimately damaging the parent-child relationship.

By shifting the focus to consistent efforts in modeling behavior and maintaining a calm, confident presence, parents can alleviate frustration. This approach encourages a more harmonious family dynamic, where children feel secure and supported. When parents demonstrate calm confidence rather than anxious control, children are more likely to respond positively. They thrive in an environment where they feel understood and respected, rather than one where they feel coerced or judged.

In summary, embracing The Dichotomy of Control allows parents to recognize the importance of their own actions and attitudes in shaping their children's development. By focusing on what they can control—such as their values, tone, and boundaries—parents can foster a sense of security and trust, ultimately guiding their children towards becoming well-adjusted individuals.

Identifying External Factors

Identifying external factors in parenting and child development is essential for grasping the complexities that shape a child's growth. While a child's unique personality influences their reactions to different situations, external elements such as social trends and peer dynamics significantly impact their development. Acknowledging these influences can help parents overcome guilt when faced with challenges in their children's lives. When parents accept that certain stressors are unavoidable, they can reduce emotional overwhelm. This understanding paves the way for a more balanced approach to parenting, allowing the focus to shift toward nurturing strengths and developing coping strategies, rather than striving to eliminate every obstacle. Embracing this perspective empowers parents to navigate their children's journeys with confidence and resilience

This perspective also enhances empathy, as it encourages parents to view their children as individuals navigating a world filled with uncontrollable variables. By understanding that children, like adults, face external pressures and influences, parents can better support them through challenges rather than feeling inadequate in their ability to provide a perfect environment.

The Stoic philosophy reinforces this mindset by emphasizing the importance of distinguishing between what can be controlled and what cannot. By focusing efforts on the aspects of parenting that are within their influence—such as providing love, support, and guidance—parents can cultivate a sense of serenity. Accepting that some factors are beyond their reach fosters resilience in both parents and children, enabling a healthier family dynamic where challenges can be faced with understanding and strength.

Aligning Intentions with Action

Aligning intentions with actions is not just a principle; it is the cornerstone of effective parenting as taught by Epictetus. The essence of successful parenting lies in having a clear purpose, grounded in a deep understanding of one's core values. When parents identify and embrace values like kindness, patience, and discipline, they create a powerful guiding compass for their behavior. Consistency is vital. When parents' actions consistently mirror their stated values, they cultivate an atmosphere of trust. Consider a parent who exemplifies patience, even in the face of challenges; this unwavering commitment reinforces the very values they wish to instill. On the other hand, inconsistency breeds confusion and can significantly erode the trust children place in their parents. Inevitably, mistakes will occur on the parenting journey. When they do, it is crucial to reflect on the gap between intentions and actions. This reflective practice not only fosters personal growth but also serves as a powerful lesson in integrity for children. When children see their parents acknowledging missteps and actively seeking improvement, they learn that making mistakes is a natural part of being human and that accountability is paramount. At its heart, the goal is to refine one's character rather than strive for an unattainable perfection in external circumstances. As Eleanor Roosevelt wisely stated, "One's philosophy is not best expressed in words; it is expressed in the choices one makes." This powerful perspective shows children that true integrity goes beyond lofty ideals; it is defined by the everyday choices that bring those ideals to life. By embracing this understanding, we instill in them the vital belief that genuine growth occurs when our intentions are in harmony with our actions. Let us empower our children to embody their values through their decisions, shaping a more authentic and principled future.

Benefits of Embracing the Dichotomy

Embracing the dichotomy of control invites parents into a transformative philosophical journey that significantly enhances their family dynamics and personal well-being. This acceptance fosters a profound reduction in anxiety. When parents relinquish the illusion of control over uncontrollable outcomes, they free themselves from the incessant worry that often clouds their judgment. The liberation from this mental burden allows for a more serene home environment, where peace of mind flourishes, creating a nurturing space for both parents and children.

Moreover, this acceptance cultivates stronger relationships. Children are remarkably perceptive; they instinctively recognize when their parents are entrapped in the web of micromanagement. By stepping back and allowing children the autonomy to navigate their own paths, parents not only foster independence but also build trust. This trust serves as the bedrock for deeper emotional connections, enabling families to engage in open dialogues where feelings and thoughts are shared freely.

Greater adaptability emerges as a natural consequence of this mindset. Life is inherently unpredictable, and when parents acknowledge that external events are beyond their control, they develop a remarkable flexibility in their responses. This adaptability becomes a model for children, who learn to embrace change and uncertainty with grace. They witness firsthand how to maintain inner peace amid the chaos of life, a skill that is invaluable in an ever-evolving world.

Furthermore, the approach to discipline transforms into a more meaningful practice. Instead of reacting with frustration to misbehavior, parents guided by principled choices can offer constructive guidance. This shift from reaction to reflection empowers parents to teach their children about consequences and values in a manner that is both compassionate and instructive. It is an opportunity for growth rather than punishment, fostering a sense of responsibility and understanding in children.

Lastly, enhanced resilience is a significant benefit of this philosophical stance. When parents model calm acceptance in the face of adversity, they imbue their children with the ability to confront setbacks with composure. Children who observe their parents navigating challenges without panic learn to internalize these lessons, building their resilience. They grow up equipped to face the inevitable trials of life with a sense of confidence and inner strength.

In embracing the dichotomy, parents not only enhance their own lives but also empower their children to become adaptable, resilient individuals capable of thriving in an unpredictable world. Such a philosophical approach does not merely reshape family dynamics; it prepares the next generation to engage with life's complexities with wisdom and grace.

Everyday Applications

Morning Check-In offers a profound opportunity to anchor ourselves in the present moment. By distinguishing between what we can control and what we cannot, we reclaim our power. Our schedules and attitudes are within our grasp, while external factors like traffic and weather remain unpredictable. This practice reminds us that our responses define our experiences, not the circumstances themselves. Embracing this philosophy can transform the mundane into a source of strength, allowing us to approach each day with intention and clarity.

Setting realistic goals is not merely a strategy for effective parenting; it is a philosophical stance that embraces the essence of human experience. In a world where perfection is often idolized, framing our day around achievable conversations with our teens fosters a more authentic connection. It acknowledges the importance of effort and understanding over unattainable ideals. By shaping our aspirations to align with reality, we cultivate resilience and nurture the potential for meaningful engagement in our relationships.

Reflecting on our triggers offers a pathway to self-discovery and growth. When we note moments of feeling out of control, we invite introspection. This reflection can guide us toward identifying aspects we can influence, shifting our focus from the uncontrollable to the controllable. Such a practice not only promotes emotional intelligence but also empowers us to navigate challenges with grace and mindfulness, illustrating the profound impact of perspective on our wellbeing.

Rewarding effort over outcomes is a radical departure from conventional notions of success. By praising children for their diligence, we instill values of perseverance and resilience. This approach fosters a growth mindset, where the journey is celebrated, and the inevitability of failure becomes a stepping stone to mastery. In this philosophical framework, we reshape our understanding of achievement, encouraging our children to embrace challenges with curiosity rather than fear.

Celebrating growth, particularly in our ability to release anxiety, is a vital acknowledgment of our journey. Each step forward, no matter how small, deserves recognition. By honoring these strides, we cultivate a culture of self-compassion and resilience, both in ourselves and in our children. This practice not only reinforces the importance of progress over perfection but also creates a supportive environment where growth is celebrated as a shared human experience. Through these principles, we weave a tapestry of mindful living that enriches our daily lives and our relationships.

Identifying Parenting Stressors
The Archer's Paradox

In Stoic philosophy, the archer embodies a profound truth: while we can hone our skills—such as stance, aim, and the release of the arrow—we cannot fully control whether the arrow hits its mark. Unexpected factors, like a sudden gust of wind or the target's movement, can alter its path. True success, therefore, lies not in the outcome but in the archer's dedication and intent.

We pour our hearts into instilling core values and building routines, yet we cannot dictate every outcome. Embracing Stoic diligence empowers us to give our all—offering unwavering support, upholding consistent discipline, and nurturing empathy—while acknowledging that our children's choices and external circumstances will shape their paths. This mindset fosters inner peace, freeing us from the burden of perfection and allowing us to trust the journey of guiding our children rather than attempting to control every aspect of it. Rather than tallying successes and failures, we focus on fulfilling our responsibilities with integrity, finding comfort in knowing we have done our utmost, even amidst the unpredictable challenges that life presents each day.

Common Sources of Anxiety

In the realm of parenting, stressors emerge as inevitable companions, weaving a complex tapestry of anxiety that can overshadow the joy of nurturing a child. Each source of stress reflects not just the realities of modern life, but also the deeper philosophical inquiries into the nature of existence, identity, and the shared human experience.

"Knowing yourself is the beginning of all wisdom." - Aristotle.

The importance of self-awareness and introspection in understanding one's place in the world. In discussing its relevance, one could explore how self-knowledge influences decision-making, relationships, and personal growth. It suggests that wisdom is not merely about acquiring knowledge but involves a deep understanding of oneself, leading to more meaningful and authentic experiences in life.

Uncertainty about a child's future looms large in the minds of parents, echoing the age-old question of what it means to guide another being through life's unpredictable journey. This anxiety is not merely a product of contemporary pressures regarding academics, career, and relationships; it is a profound reflection on the nature of control and the limits of parental influence. As parents, we grapple with the weight of our hopes and dreams for our children, often clashing with the stark reality that the future is inherently uncertain, a realm that no amount of preparation can fully navigate.

The pervasive influence of social media introduces another layer to this anxiety. In a world where curated images of 'ideal parenting' flood our feeds, the instinct to compare ourselves to others becomes almost instinctual. This social comparison, fraught with the peril of perceived societal judgments, forces us to confront our own insecurities. It raises philosophical questions about authenticity, self-worth, and the societal constructs of success. Are we measuring our parenting against a fleeting ideal that is itself a façade?

Financial and temporal constraints further complicate the quest for ideal parenting. The relentless pursuit of resources often leads to an existential crisis, where the disparity between aspiration and reality breeds feelings of inadequacy. This struggle invites a reflection on the nature of fulfillment and the societal definitions of success. It challenges us to question whether the 'ideal' is a tangible goal or a mirage, forever elusive in the face of life's harsh realities.

Conflicts with co-parents or extended family often serve as a mirror, reflecting not only differing philosophies of child-rearing but also the intricacies of human relationships. These conflicts compel us to explore the nature of collaboration and compromise within the familial sphere. They prompt a deeper inquiry into our values and the collective responsibility we bear in shaping the lives of the next generation. Each disagreement is not merely a challenge but an opportunity to engage in a dialogue about love, support, and the shared journey of parenting.

Finally, the specter of one's unresolved emotional baggage surfaces under the weight of stress, revealing the profound interconnectedness of our personal histories with our present roles. This aspect of parenting compels us to acknowledge that our emotional landscapes—shaped by past experiences—inform our interactions with our children. It invites us to embark on a journey of self-discovery, emphasizing the importance of healing and understanding as we strive to offer our children a nurturing environment.

In essence, identifying parenting stressors transcends mere acknowledgment; it is an invitation to engage in a philosophical exploration of our own identities, values, and the societal constructs that shape our experiences. Through this lens, we may find not only the sources of our anxiety but also pathways toward greater understanding and resilience in the art of parenting.

Control vs. Influence

In the delicate interplay between control and influence, one must consider the profound implications of each approach on the development of the child. Control, often rooted in a desire for order and predictability, can inadvertently cultivate an atmosphere of resistance. When parents or guardians impose their will too rigidly, the natural response from a child may be rebellion, a manifestation of the innate human desire for autonomy. Alternatively, excessive control can engender dependency, stifling the very independence that is essential for healthy maturation.

Influence, however, stands as a more nuanced and respectful interaction. It acknowledges the agency of the child while providing guidance and setting essential boundaries that ensure safety and moral development. This approach fosters cooperation, as children learn to engage with their environment and the expectations set before them. When parents offer influence rather than control, they invite dialogue and understanding, cultivating an atmosphere rich in mutual respect.

This dynamic resonates with Stoic philosophy, which advocates for moderation in all things. Stoicism teaches us to navigate the extremes of neglect and authoritarianism, urging us toward a balanced middle path. This equilibrium nurtures the child's sense of agency while providing the necessary structure for growth. In this space of moderation, children can flourish, developing the skills to make choices that reflect their values and understanding of the world.

Trust emerges as a cornerstone of this relationship. When children perceive that their autonomy is honored, they are more likely to engage openly with their caregivers. Such trust creates a fertile ground for personal development, where children feel empowered to explore their identities while knowing they have a supportive framework to rely upon. In this light, the act of influencing becomes a sacred responsibility; it is a means of guiding rather than dictating, shaping rather than controlling. Thus, the philosophy of influence, steeped in understanding and respect, not only enriches the child's experience but also cultivates a profound bond of trust and cooperation between parent and child.

Tools for Identifying Stress

In the realm of parenting, where emotions ebb and flow like the tides, the exploration of stress and anxiety becomes a profound philosophical inquiry. Journaling serves as an intimate dialogue with oneself, allowing the parent to articulate and confront the complexities of their emotional landscape. By documenting triggers of anxiety or frustration, one engages in a reflective practice that transcends mere record-keeping; it becomes a quest for understanding the self and the intricate web of parenting experiences. This act transforms ephemeral feelings into tangible words, inviting the parent to confront the underlying beliefs and fears that may be shaping their reactions.

Mindful observation introduces a moment of pause, a sacred space in the chaotic rhythm of parenting. It poses a critical question: "Is this truly within my control?" This inquiry aligns with existential thought, inviting parents to discern between the chaos they can influence and that which lies beyond their grasp. In this moment, one may begin to untangle the threads of responsibility, recognizing that the emotional turmoil often stems from a misguided sense of control. Here, the philosophy of acceptance can take root, encouraging a surrender to the reality of life's unpredictability, which is especially poignant in the context of nurturing another human being.

The act of conversation, whether with a trusted friend or a therapist, embodies the human need for connection and understanding. In sharing anxieties, parents engage in a communal act of vulnerability, revealing the universal nature of their struggles. This exchange can foster a sense of solidarity, reminding individuals that the burdens they carry are not borne in isolation but are part of a shared human experience. Such dialogues elevate the act of parenting from a solitary endeavor to a collective journey, where wisdom and comfort can be found in the shared acknowledgment of challenges.

Self-awareness apps represent the intersection of technology and self-exploration, offering a modern avenue for introspection. By tracking moods and identifying patterns, these tools facilitate a deeper understanding of stressors, transforming abstract feelings into quantifiable data. Philosophically, this raises questions about the nature of self-knowledge in an age dominated by digital interfaces. While such applications provide insights, they also challenge the parent to consider the extent to which technology can enhance, or perhaps complicate, the journey toward self-awareness.

Lastly, support systems emerge as a vital component of navigating the labyrinth of parenting stress. Engaging with fellow parents can illuminate the shared nature of stressors, fostering a sense of normalcy amid individual chaos. This collective insight serves as a reminder that while each parenting experience is unique, the feelings of anxiety and frustration are often universal. Philosophically, this reinforces the notion that our struggles, though deeply personal, are interwoven with the fabric of human experience, inviting a deeper exploration of empathy and understanding within the parenting community.

In summary, the tools for identifying stress in parenting encourage a philosophical examination of self, connection, and the shared nature of human experience. Through journaling, mindful observation, conversation, technology, and community, parents are invited to embark on a journey of discovery, not only of their own emotional landscapes but also of the intricate connections that bind them to others navigating the same path.

Psychological Perspectives

Cognitive-behavioral theory posits that distorted beliefs about control can significantly inflate stress levels. This notion resonates deeply within the realm of parenting, where the balance between nurturing and guiding often tips into the territory of excessive control. When parents harbor distorted perceptions—believing that every outcome in their child's life rests solely upon their shoulders—their anxiety can manifest in overbearing behaviors, stifling the very independence they seek to cultivate. In this light, relinquishing the illusion of control becomes not just a path to personal peace but also a gift to the child, allowing them to encounter life's uncertainties and develop resilience.

Self-efficacy research further illuminates the psychological landscape of parenting. The belief in one's own capabilities to adapt fosters a sense of confidence that can ripple through familial relationships. Parents who embody this confidence create an environment where children feel safe to explore and confront challenges. Rather than succumbing to panic in the face of adversity, both parent and child can approach difficulties as opportunities for growth. Thus, instilling a sense of self-efficacy in children becomes an essential task, nurturing their ability to navigate life's complexities with assurance.

Attachment theory offers profound insights into the dynamics of parent-child relationships. The construct of a "secure base" underscores the importance of emotional safety in fostering a child's exploration of the world. Children flourish when they perceive their parents not as authoritarian figures but as supportive allies. This secure attachment allows children to venture into the unknown, knowing they can return to a nurturing presence. The philosophical implication here is that love and guidance should coexist, allowing autonomy to blossom rather than imposing control that breeds fear and compliance.

Emotional intelligence models contribute another critical dimension to this discourse. The ability to understand and navigate one's own emotional landscape is essential for effective parenting. When parents possess emotional intelligence, they can respond to their children's emotional needs with empathy and clarity, rather than reacting impulsively or overwhelming them with their own emotional turmoil. This understanding fosters a calm atmosphere, where children learn not just to identify their feelings but also to manage them constructively.

The integration of Stoic concepts with these psychological frameworks introduces a holistic, balanced approach to parenting. Stoicism teaches the value of distinguishing between what is within our control and what is not, a lesson that resonates profoundly in the parenting domain. By embracing this philosophy, parents can cultivate an attitude of equanimity, focusing on their role in guiding without overstepping into the realm of control. This balance encourages children to take ownership of their experiences, fostering resilience and adaptability.

Ultimately, the philosophical underpinnings of these psychological perspectives advocate for a parenting style that values autonomy, emotional insight, and a supportive foundation. Such an approach recognizes the intricate dance between guidance and freedom, allowing children to grow into capable individuals who navigate the complexities of life with confidence and grace.

Channeling Stress into Constructive Action

Channeling stress into constructive action invites a philosophical exploration of human resilience and the transformative power of adversity. The act of identifying practical steps, such as scheduling quiet time to decompress, reflects a fundamental understanding of the need for balance in a world often characterized by chaos. This acknowledgment of quietude serves as a sanctuary for the mind, a necessary retreat that allows individuals to confront the root causes of their stress rather than merely addressing its symptoms.

Engaging children in problem-solving fosters a collaborative spirit that transforms stress-inducing situations into fertile ground for growth. This practice not only empowers children to confront challenges with agency but also instills in them a philosophical appreciation for the complexities of life. It teaches that difficulties are not merely obstacles but opportunities for learning and development, thus creating a shared narrative that unites family members in their collective journey.

Building a contingency plan for repeated stressors, such as the familiar morning chaos or homework struggles, embodies a proactive approach to life's uncertainties. It acknowledges the cyclical nature of stressors and encourages a mindset that prepares for, rather than dreads, their inevitable return. This foresight reflects a deeper philosophical inquiry into the nature of existence, where acceptance of life's unpredictability can lead to a more resilient and harmonious family dynamic.

Practicing cognitive reframing invites a shift in perspective that enhances our understanding of challenges. Viewing these obstacles as chances to strengthen family bonds transforms stress into a catalyst for connection. This philosophical lens encourages a deeper exploration of the relationships we cultivate, suggesting that through shared struggles, families can forge stronger ties and develop a profound appreciation for one another's strengths and vulnerabilities.

Celebrating small victories serves as a reminder that progress is often incremental, a series of small steps that collectively lead to greater resilience. This practice nurtures a sense of accomplishment that is vital in the face of life's persistent challenges. It encourages a philosophical reflection on the nature of success, emphasizing that each overcome stressor, no matter how minor, contributes to a larger narrative of growth and fortitude. Through this lens, individuals and families can find meaning in their experiences, cultivating a sense of purpose that transcends the immediate discomfort of stress.

Strategies to Let Go of Anxiety

Acceptance as an Active Process

Acceptance is not just a passive resignation; it is a bold, conscious decision to face reality head-on, unclouded by denial. As Alan Watts wisely stated, "The only way to make sense out of change is to plunge into it, move with it, and join the dance." This powerful perspective reveals a profound truth: true strength does not come from attempting to control every outcome, but from embracing a fluid and intentional response to life's uncertainties. Choose to accept and engage with the world as it is, and watch how it transforms your experience.

By surrendering the illusion of total control, we liberate our minds from the shackles of anxiety, thereby creating cognitive space to focus on what is actionable. When we teach children that feeling disappointment or frustration is a natural part of existence, we equip them with the tools to navigate a world rife with unpredictability. It is vital to instill in them the understanding that dwelling on what is beyond their control is ultimately unproductive. Instead, we can guide them toward recognizing their feelings, processing them, and then letting them go.

Acceptance does not negate effort; rather, it complements it. We can strive to do our best within the parameters of what we can influence—our actions, our attitudes, our responses—while simultaneously releasing the need to control the outcomes. This balance fosters a healthier mindset, allowing both parents and children to cultivate emotional resilience over time. By embracing acceptance as an active process, we empower ourselves and the next generation to face life's challenges with grace and fortitude, transforming anxiety into a source of strength rather than a hindrance.

Breathing and Mindfulness Techniques

Breathing and mindfulness techniques serve as profound gateways to self-awareness and tranquility, inviting us to explore the intricate relationship between body and mind. Box breathing, with its structured rhythm of inhale, hold, exhale, and pause, embodies a cyclical pattern that mirrors the natural ebb and flow of existence. This practice not only calms the nervous system but also illustrates the philosophical principle of balance—the equilibrium between action and stillness, engagement and detachment.

The body scan invites an intimate dialogue with oneself, urging a gentle exploration from head to toe. In this act of mental check-in, we confront the corporeal manifestations of stress and anxiety, fostering a deeper understanding of the self. This technique underscores the philosophical notion of embodiment, positing that our minds are inextricably linked to our physical states. By releasing tension, we do not merely alleviate discomfort; we engage in a transformative process that reconnects us with the present, enhancing our overall awareness.

Guided imagery, the art of visualizing serene landscapes, serves as an antidote to the relentless currents of anxiety. Within the confines of our minds, we construct sanctuaries that allow us to transcend the chaos of the external world. This practice echoes philosophical ideas about the power of imagination and the subjective nature of reality, suggesting that our perceptions can shape our experiences. In visualizing tranquility, we cultivate a mental refuge, offering respite from the tumultuous nature of life.

Mindful observation, the act of acknowledging thoughts without judgment, reflects a profound acceptance of the human condition. This practice invites us to recognize the transient nature of thoughts, akin to clouds drifting across the sky. By reframing our relationship with our internal dialogue, we embody the philosophical stance of non-attachment. In releasing our need to control or suppress thoughts, we embrace the present moment, finding freedom in acceptance rather than resistance.

Integrating these practices into daily routines or during conflict moments becomes an act of intentional living. In a world often characterized by haste and distraction, these techniques remind us of the value of presence. They encourage a philosophical inquiry into the nature of our responses to life's challenges, urging us to cultivate composure and clarity. Through the conscious incorporation of breathing and mindfulness, we embark on a journey of self-discovery, resilience, and ultimately, a deeper connection to the essence of being.

Stoic Reflection Exercises

In the realm of Stoic thought, the practice of reflection serves as a vital tool for cultivating resilience and fortitude in the face of life's inevitable challenges. The exercise of Premeditation Malorum invites individuals to momentarily engage with the specter of adversity, considering the potential disruptions that may surface in daily life, whether they be familial discord or the trivial yet frustrating experience of a missed school bus. This contemplation is not an act of pessimism but rather a proactive strategy to fortify the mind against the disturbances that life may present. By anticipating these difficulties, one can approach them with a sense of preparedness, thereby mitigating their emotional impact.

Negative Visualization extends this concept further, urging individuals to envision the loss of what they hold dear. This exercise may evoke discomfort, yet it serves an essential purpose: to deepen appreciation for the present moment and the relationships and possessions that enrich our existence. In acknowledging the transitory nature of life, we cultivate a profound sense of gratitude, which can, in turn, enhance our emotional resilience. By recognizing that loss is an inherent aspect of existence, we learn to cherish more fully what we have while remaining emotionally equipped to handle potential sorrow.

The focus on virtue amidst life's trials is a cornerstone of Stoic philosophy. By asking oneself which virtues—be it patience, wisdom, or courage—may be exercised in the face of a particular scenario, one redirects attention from external circumstances to internal character. This introspection fosters a proactive mindset, encouraging individuals to respond to challenges not with frustration or despair but with a commitment to personal growth and ethical conduct. It is through this lens that we can transform adversity into an opportunity for the cultivation of virtue.

The Daily Review acts as a reflective mirror, allowing for an honest assessment of one's responses throughout the day. In this practice, one examines moments of composure against those of faltering, creating a space for self-improvement and mindful awareness. Such reflection is not merely a means of self-critique but an essential process of learning and adaptation. It reinforces the understanding that the path to virtue is not linear but rather a series of trials and triumphs that shape our character.

Collectively, these Stoic reflection exercises sharpen one's awareness and prepare the mind for the unpredictability of life. By engaging in these practices, individuals cultivate a sense of equanimity that guards against the panic that often accompanies unforeseen challenges. In the Stoic view, it is not the events themselves that dictate our emotional state, but our interpretation and response to them that ultimately define our experience. Through these exercises, we forge a resilient spirit capable of navigating the complexities of existence with grace and wisdom.

Releasing Control Without Neglecting Responsibility

Releasing control is a profound act of trust, both in ourselves and in our children. It requires us to navigate the delicate balance between guiding and protecting, while also allowing for personal growth and autonomy. Letting go of anxiety does not equate to neglecting our responsibilities as caregivers or guardians. Instead, it invites us to embrace a more enlightened form of parenting—one rooted in calm discernment rather than fear and overreach.

Setting boundaries and providing structure are essential components of responsible guidance. However, the manner in which we establish these boundaries can radically influence the developmental landscape of our children. When we approach these boundaries from a place of calmness, we communicate strength and stability, fostering an environment where children feel secure enough to explore and express themselves. This sense of security is crucial; it allows them to engage with the world while knowing they have a safety net to fall back on.

Moreover, focusing on teaching principles such as honesty and perseverance rather than micromanaging every outcome empowers children to internalize these values. Life is fraught with challenges, and it is essential that children learn to navigate them independently. By emphasizing principles, we cultivate resilience and character, allowing them to make choices that align with these values. This process is not merely about avoiding mistakes; it is about cultivating wisdom through experience.

Open communication about expectations and consequences is another cornerstone of this balanced approach. By articulating these aspects clearly, we establish a framework that children can understand and respect. This transparency fosters a sense of accountability; children learn that their choices have real implications. Yet, within this framework, they are given the freedom to explore their own paths. This not only nurtures their decision-making skills but also instills a deep-rooted sense of responsibility for their actions.

As we implement this balanced approach, we inadvertently build a relationship founded on mutual respect. Children who feel trusted are more likely to engage openly and honestly with their parents. They learn that their thoughts and feelings matter, which encourages them to express themselves freely and seek guidance when needed. This connection creates a partnership where both parties feel valued and understood, dismantling the authoritarian dynamic that often stifles growth.

Ultimately, releasing control while maintaining responsibility is an invitation for both parents and children to grow together. It is a journey towards fostering autonomy, accountability, and mutual respect, essential qualities for navigating life's complexities. Let us embrace this approach, recognizing that the greatest gift we can offer our children is not a world devoid of challenges, but the tools and confidence to face those challenges with grace and integrity.

Seeking Professional or Community Support

In the journey of life, the weight of anxiety can often feel insurmountable, shrouding our clarity and stifling our potential. However, seeking professional or community support emerges as a beacon of hope—a vital step towards reclaiming one's well-being. As we navigate this complex emotional landscape, we must recognize that therapy or counseling is not merely an avenue for relief; it is a gateway to acquiring invaluable coping tools. These tools empower us to confront our anxieties with resilience, illustrating the profound truth that "The greatest weapon against stress is our ability to choose one thought over another."

Engaging in parenting workshops or Stoic-based discussion groups introduces us to fresh perspectives that can radically alter our approach to life's challenges. Stoicism teaches us to embrace what we cannot control and focus on our responses to it. In these gatherings, we find camaraderie among those who share similar struggles, which normalizes our challenges and fosters an environment ripe for growth. The act of sharing insights with like-minded peers cannot be overstated; it creates a collective wisdom that lightens the burden of our individual experiences.

Moreover, the importance of a support network cannot be overlooked. Such a network serves as a vital mechanism for accountability, encouraging us to maintain healthy mental habits that might otherwise falter under the pressure of anxiety. It is within this circle of support that we discover not only encouragement but also the strength to pursue our journey with intention and purpose. As we remind ourselves, "Asking for help demonstrates strength, not weakness." This shift in perspective is crucial; it transforms the act of seeking assistance into a declaration of our commitment to personal growth and resilience.

In a world that often promotes the illusion of self-sufficiency, let us embrace the truth that vulnerability is a source of strength. By reaching out, we not only enhance our own lives but also inspire those around us to do the same. In this interconnected tapestry of human experience, each thread contributes to a richer, more supportive community. Thus, let us not shy away from seeking the help we need; instead, let us boldly step forward, equipped with the understanding that true strength lies in our willingness to connect, share, and grow together.

Replacing Worry with Constructive Action
Turning Worry into Problem-Solving

Replacing worry with constructive action embodies a profound shift in our approach to life's challenges. The act of worrying, often rooted in anxiety and uncertainty, can lead individuals into a labyrinth of hypothetical dilemmas. Instead of succumbing to this mental quagmire, one can embrace the philosophy of proactive engagement, transforming worry into a catalyst for problem-solving.

As Albert Camus once said, "Life is a sum of all your choices." This profound quote encapsulates the very essence of agency in our lives and emphasizes the importance of decision-making. When faced with the academic struggles of a child, for example, it becomes imperative to navigate away from the paralyzing "what if?" scenarios that often cloud our judgment. Instead, we should focus on making deliberate choices that actively foster growth and learning. Establishing a structured study schedule or seeking out the guidance of a tutor represents not just a response to anxiety, but a powerful affirmation of our commitment to improvement and progress. These choices can create a supportive environment that nurtures resilience and encourages a positive approach to challenges.

By channeling emotional energy into concrete actions, we not only lighten the burdens we carry but also cultivate resilience within ourselves and our children. Teaching children the art of problem-solving instills in them a can-do attitude that transcends the confines of fear. They learn that challenges are not insurmountable obstacles but opportunities for growth and understanding.

Moreover, engaging in practical steps fosters a sense of accomplishment. Each small victory reinforces self-efficacy, empowering individuals to confront future challenges with renewed vigor. In this way, the act of transforming worry into action becomes a profound exercise in courage and agency, allowing us to navigate the vicissitudes of life with a spirit of resolve and optimism.

Collaborative Family Planning

Collaborative family planning represents a transformative approach to familial dynamics, one that transcends mere compliance and fosters a sense of shared responsibility. Involving children in the creation of routines, chore lists, or conflict-resolution strategies cultivates an environment where expectations are clear and ownership is shared. This collaborative framework not only diminishes tension within the family unit but also nurtures an atmosphere of mutual respect and understanding.

When children participate in setting the rules and expectations, they gain insight into the rationale behind them. This engagement cultivates a deeper comprehension of the family's collective goals and values. They learn that their contributions matter, which instills a sense of agency and empowerment. In this shared space, negotiation becomes a vital skill, where children learn to articulate their needs and listen to others, fostering empathy as they recognize that their perspectives are part of a broader dialogue.

Moreover, the act of communal goal-setting reinforces the idea that challenges are best faced together. Families can tackle obstacles collaboratively, reinforcing the notion that support and teamwork are fundamental to overcoming difficulties. This process not only strengthens familial bonds but also equips children with the life skills they will carry into adulthood. They learn time management as they juggle responsibilities, and through the negotiation of chores or resolving conflicts, they develop critical thinking and problem-solving abilities.

As children grow within this collaborative framework, they transition from being passive recipients of rules to proactive contributors to the family structure. This evolution is crucial; it prepares them for future endeavors in various contexts—academic, social, and professional. They will emerge as individuals who understand the value of collaboration, equipped with the tools to engage effectively within any community.

In essence, embracing collaborative family planning is not merely an organizational strategy; it is a philosophical commitment to nurturing well-rounded individuals who appreciate the dynamics of collective effort. It is about cultivating a family culture where every member's voice is valued, creating a harmonious environment that fosters growth, understanding, and resilience in the face of life's challenges.

Harnessing the Power of Ritual.

Rituals serve as the quiet backbone of human experience, providing structure and meaning in a world often characterized by chaos and uncertainty. The simple act of engaging in daily rituals, such as a brief morning gratitude practice, can cultivate an environment of reflection and appreciation within the family unit. This practice not only centers the individual but also creates a ripple effect, anchoring the collective mindset of the family.

Family dinners, as a ritual, transcend mere sustenance; they evolve into a sacred space where individuals can articulate their highs and lows. This sharing fosters emotional intimacy, allowing family members to connect on a deeper level. In this exchange, there exists a profound acknowledgment of each other's experiences, nurturing empathy and reinforcing the bonds that tie individuals together. The act of gathering around a table transforms into a ritual of unity, where the mundane becomes meaningful.

In a world rife with unpredictability, rituals act as a stabilizing force. They introduce a sense of predictability that can alleviate anxiety, reminding us of the constancy that can exist amidst the turmoil. Each ritual, whether grand or simple, provides a framework within which individuals can find solace and security. This predictability fosters a sense of belonging, as individuals come to anticipate and rely on these shared moments.

Moreover, the repeated enactment of rituals instills core values within the family. Respect, gratitude, and teamwork are not merely abstract ideals but are embodied in the practices that families adopt. Over time, these shared habits cultivate a culture of mindfulness and discipline, echoing the Stoic philosophy that emphasizes the importance of inner strength and self-control. Through the lens of Stoicism, rituals become not just habits, but exercises in virtue, guiding individuals toward a life of intentionality and purpose.

In essence, rituals encapsulate the delicate interplay between individual and collective experiences. They remind us that within the rhythm of daily life, there lies the potential for profound connection and growth.

By embracing rituals, families can navigate the complexities of existence with greater resilience, finding meaning in both the ordinary and the extraordinary.

Turning Mistakes into Lessons

Turning mistakes into lessons is a profound philosophical stance that invites one to reconsider the nature of errors in the human experience. Within the Stoic framework, errors are not viewed as definitive failures but rather as necessary components of the journey toward wisdom. This perspective reframes missteps, such as a poor choice made at school, as invaluable opportunities for growth and learning.

In guiding children to understand this concept, it is essential to approach their missteps with gentleness, fostering an environment where they can reflect on their decisions without fear of harsh judgment. By cultivating a mindset that sees errors as integral to the learning process, we can help them recognize that each mistake is a stepping stone, a moment that contributes to their evolving understanding of themselves and the world around them.

Modeling self-forgiveness serves as a powerful example for children. When adults acknowledge their own emotional reactions or failures in a calm and reflective manner, they demonstrate that it is possible to embrace imperfection. This not only reinforces the importance of resilience but also highlights the value of self-compassion. By discussing strategies for handling similar situations with more composure in the future, we reinforce the notion that growth is a continuous journey, rather than a destination marked by flawless performance.

This philosophical approach liberates the household from the paralyzing fear of failure. In an atmosphere where experimentation is encouraged and reflection is valued, children learn to navigate challenges with curiosity rather than dread. They come to understand that each mistake is not a mark against their character but rather an opportunity to cultivate wisdom and deepen their understanding. Thus, the household becomes a space of exploration, where lessons abound and the path to personal growth is paved with the understanding that errors are not the end, but the beginning of a richer, more profound journey.

Building Confidence Through Consistency

Building confidence through consistency is not merely a suggestion; it is a profound necessity in the development of emotional fortitude. In an age where uncertainty looms large, the power of consistent, constructive actions emerges as a beacon of stability. By choosing to engage in actions that are deliberate and positive, rather than succumbing to the paralyzing grip of worry, we empower ourselves and those around us, particularly children, to cultivate resilience.

Children flourish in environments characterized by consistent leadership. When they know what to expect and can trust the guidance of their parents or caregivers, they are more likely to explore, take risks, and ultimately grow. This framework of reliability fosters a sense of safety, allowing children to navigate the complexities of their world with confidence. Each instance of consistency sends a clear message: rational effort leads to tangible results. This affirmation, whether it manifests in small victories or significant achievements, reinforces the notion that they have agency over their lives.

Over time, this cultivation of success transforms the emotional landscape of the family. Anxiety, which often feels like an ever-present shadow, begins to recede, replaced by a burgeoning confidence that becomes the family's default mode of operation. As this shift occurs, both parents and children develop a sense of mastery over life's inevitable ups and downs. They learn that challenges are not insurmountable obstacles but opportunities for growth and learning.

In embracing consistency, we not only nurture our own confidence but also lay the groundwork for future generations to thrive. The cycle of empowerment continues as children internalize these lessons, becoming resilient adults capable of facing life's uncertainties with courage and assurance. Thus, by committing to consistent, constructive actions, we forge a path toward a more confident and capable family dynamic, one where worry has no place and mastery becomes the norm.

Cultivating a Growth Mindset in the Family
Why a Growth Mindset Matter.

A growth mindset matters profoundly within the family dynamic, as it shapes not only individual development but also the collective spirit of familial bonds. Psychologist Carol Dweck's research illuminates the transformative power of perceiving abilities as malleable, stating, "The view you adopt for yourself profoundly affects the way you lead your life." This perspective encourages not just persistence in the face of challenges but also resilience, allowing individuals to embrace failures as stepping stones rather than insurmountable obstacles.

In the realm of philosophy, Stoics like Marcus Aurelius echoed this sentiment, viewing life as an ongoing journey of self-improvement. Aurelius noted, "The impediment to action advances action. What stands in the way becomes the way." This Stoic principle reinforces the idea that each challenge presents a unique opportunity to cultivate virtue and refine character, mirroring the essence of a growth mindset.

By fostering an environment that prioritizes growth over perfection, families can alleviate the burdens of unrealistic expectations. A growth mindset reduces the pressure of perfectionism, offering children the space to evolve at their own pace. As Dweck articulates, "When we are in a growth mindset, we are motivated by challenges." This motivation nurtures a sense of curiosity and a willingness to explore, essential traits in a rapidly changing world.

Moreover, this philosophy extends to parenting itself, framing it as a skill that is not fixed but continually evolving. Parents, too, grow and learn through their experiences, embodying the very principles they wish to instill in their children. The realization that "parenting is a journey, not a destination" allows for greater flexibility and understanding within family relationships.

Emphasizing progress over innate talent shifts the focus from mere achievement to genuine development. This mindset cultivates long-term success and adaptability, preparing children not only for academic endeavors but for life's myriad challenges. As John Dewey wisely said, "Education is not preparation for life; education is life itself." In embracing a growth mindset, families embark on a shared journey of learning and growth, nurturing individuals who are equipped to navigate an unpredictable future with confidence and resilience.

Connecting Growth Mindset to Stoic Principles

Growth mindset and Stoic principles converge beautifully in their shared emphasis on effort, resilience, and ongoing self-improvement. Both philosophies advocate for the understanding that challenges are not obstacles but rather opportunities for growth. By embracing difficulties, children can cultivate a mindset that values learning from adversity, which is essential for personal development.

Encouraging children to welcome challenges is akin to the Stoic practice of facing discomfort with courage. When a child faces a setback, such as losing a soccer game or receiving a poor grade on a test, it is vital to frame these experiences as arenas for self-improvement. Rather than shying away from disappointment, children should be taught to confront it head-on, recognizing that every struggle provides a lesson. This perspective fosters resilience, enabling them to adapt and thrive in the face of future difficulties.

It is equally important to reassure children that their mistakes do not define them. What truly shapes character is how they respond to those mistakes. The Stoic philosopher Epictetus famously stated that it is not the events themselves that disturb us, but our judgments about those events. By instilling this understanding, children can learn to view failures as stepping stones rather than stumbling blocks. This notion aligns perfectly with a growth mindset, where effort and perseverance are recognized as the cornerstones of achievement.

Reinforcing the idea that adopting a growth mindset is synonymous with living virtuously and purposefully can further empower children. Virtue in Stoicism is about striving for excellence in character and action. When children embrace a growth mindset, they actively engage in the pursuit of knowledge and self-betterment, aligning their actions with the virtues of wisdom, courage, and resilience. This holistic approach not only prepares them for life's inevitable challenges but also cultivates a sense of purpose, guiding them toward a fulfilling and meaningful existence.

In summary, the connection between growth mindset and Stoic principles offers a profound framework for teaching children about resilience and personal development. By welcoming challenges, learning from setbacks, and understanding that their responses shape their character, children can navigate life's complexities with courage and virtue.

Incorporating Daily Encouragement

Complimenting children on their effort, strategy, or perseverance rather than solely on results is a profound choice that shapes their understanding of success and failure. When we acknowledge the journey rather than just the destination, we teach children that learning is a process, not a mere checklist of achievements. Each time we affirm their efforts, we instill in them the belief that their value lies not in the accolades they receive but in the resilience they demonstrate.

Consider the simple act of recognizing small wins, such as attempting a new hobby. It is crucial to celebrate these moments, even if immediate mastery is absent. By doing so, we communicate that exploration and courage are worthy pursuits in their own right. This perspective allows children to embrace challenges, nurturing a mindset where trying something new is a victory in itself, regardless of the outcome.

Specific feedback further enriches this nurturing environment. When we say, "I love how you tried different approaches to solve that puzzle," we direct their attention to the various strategies they employed. This not only validates their creative thinking but also encourages them to reflect on their methods, thereby fostering a deeper understanding of problem-solving. In focusing on the process and the thought behind their actions, we cultivate analytical skills that serve them far beyond the immediate task.

By maintaining this emphasis on learning and self-improvement, we alleviate the burdens of performance anxiety that often plague young minds. Children who feel the weight of needing to achieve perfection may shy away from challenges altogether, fearing failure more than they desire growth. However, when we shift the narrative to one of effort, we empower them to take risks, knowing that every attempt is a stepping stone toward mastery.

Over time, this approach cultivates intrinsic motivation. When children learn to find joy in their efforts and the progress they make, they become self-driven learners, eager to pursue their interests without the constant need for external validation. They begin to understand that the path to success is paved with persistence and creativity, not just the final outcome. In this way, we foster not only skilled individuals but also resilient, adaptable, and passionate learners who will carry these values into adulthood. Thus, by focusing on effort, strategy, and perseverance, we plant the seeds for a lifetime of growth, fulfillment, and a profound appreciation for the learning journey itself.

Modeling Lifelong Learning

Modeling lifelong learning is not merely an act of personal development; it is a profound demonstration of the human capacity for growth and transformation that we owe to the younger generations. When children observe adults engaging in the pursuit of new skills or facing personal challenges, they are not just passive witnesses; they are absorbing a powerful lesson in resilience and adaptability.

Sharing experiences of mistakes and outlining plans for improvement fosters an environment where imperfection is not feared but embraced. It teaches children that failure is not an endpoint but rather a stepping stone to greater understanding and mastery. This candidness cultivates a culture of openness, where the process of learning is valued over the mere attainment of success.

Engaging in activities such as reading, picking up new hobbies, or adhering to an exercise regimen embodies active self-growth. These pursuits demonstrate that learning is a lifelong journey, not confined to the walls of a classroom or the early years of life. When children see adults prioritizing their own development, they internalize the belief that they too can and should strive for growth throughout their lives.

This dynamic creates a powerful synergy within the household, reinforcing the idea that everyone is on a continuous path of learning. In this environment, curiosity flourishes, and the pursuit of knowledge becomes a shared family value. Children raised in such an ethos are more likely to embrace opportunities for self-growth, understanding that learning is a continuous, enriching experience that enhances their lives.

In conclusion, the act of modeling lifelong learning is an ethical responsibility we carry as adults. By actively pursuing our own growth and sharing our journeys, we inspire the next generation to remain open to learning, fostering a legacy of curiosity and resilience that will serve them throughout their lives.

Resilient Mindsets for the Future

A family culture that honors growth over fixed achievement stands the test of time, embodying the essence of resilience in the face of life's uncertainties. As the philosopher Heraclitus aptly stated, "The only constant in life is change." This insight underlines the importance of nurturing a mindset that embraces evolution rather than clinging to static notions of success. When children are taught to adapt to failure, they cultivate a resilience that transforms setbacks into opportunities for growth. This perspective echoes the sentiment of psychologist Carol Dweck, who asserts, "In a growth mindset, challenges are exciting rather than threatening." Thus, fostering an environment where effort and perseverance are valued over mere outcomes prepares children to navigate the complexities of life.

Moreover, the notion that parents need not possess all the answers is liberating. It encourages a shared journey of discovery, where learning becomes a collaborative endeavor. As the philosopher Jean-Paul Sartre observed, "Man is condemned to be free." This freedom to explore uncertainties alongside their children fosters deeper connections and mutual respect. Parents who model this growth-oriented mindset demonstrate that learning is a lifelong pursuit, reinforcing the idea that knowledge is not a destination but a continuous journey.

The Stoic acceptance of change aligns with the growth mindset's optimism, forming a robust foundation for resilience. Carl Jung, a groundbreaking psychologist, noted, "I am not what happened to me, I am what I choose to become." This viewpoint urges families to emphasize their reactions to life's obstacles rather than the obstacles themselves. By nurturing emotional resilience, families can confront adversity with a sense of purpose and flexibility.

Fostering this outlook prepares families for the inevitable changes and challenges that life brings. The interplay of acceptance and optimism creates a robust foundation for navigating life's unpredictability. As the poet Rainer Maria Rilke wisely noted, "The only journey is the one within." Embracing this internal journey enables families to thrive amidst external uncertainties, nurturing a resilient mindset that not only survives but flourishes in the face of change. In doing so, families establish a legacy that transcends fleeting achievements, celebrating the enduring power of growth and collaboration.

Key Takeaways (Chapter Cheat Sheet)

1. Release the Illusion of Total Control

    ◦ Epictetus's dichotomy of control reminds us to focus on our judgments and actions, not on uncontrollable externals.
2. Identify and Manage Anxiety Triggers

- Acknowledge common stressors (like social expectations) and apply Stoic and psychological tools to cope.
3. Accept, Then Act

    - Acceptance isn't passive. Recognize what you cannot change, then channel your energy into proactive solutions.
4. Constructive Action Over Worry

    - Turn anxious thoughts into practical steps—problem-solving, rituals, collaborative family planning.
5. Growth Mindset Aligns with Stoic Wisdom

    - Encourage continuous learning and self-improvement, both for yourself and your children.

Reflection Prompts

1. Journaling Exercise

    - Identify one parenting worry that regularly weighs on you (e.g., your child's future career or academic success). Which parts are within your control, and which are outside it? How might acceptance of the uncontrollable aspects reduce your stress?
2. Family Discussion

    - Discuss with your child or partner a time when you tried too hard to control an outcome. What could you have done differently? How can you apply a growth mindset in similar future situations?

3. Action Step

- Practice Epictetus's advice today: For each stress-inducing event, pause and ask, "Is this within my control?" If yes, take one proactive step. If no, consciously release it and direct your energy elsewhere.

By acknowledging the dichotomy of control, you free yourself from the burden of unrealistic expectations. This shift not only reduces parental anxiety but also fosters a more open and secure environment where children can grow. In the next chapter, we'll delve deeper into "Leading by Example: Embodying Virtue, Discipline, and Self-Control." You'll discover how embodying Stoic principles in your daily conduct can profoundly shape your children's character and set them up for a lifetime of resilience and integrity.

Three

Leading by Example

"*Waste no more time arguing about what a good man should be. Be one.*"
— *Marcus Aurelius*

Marcus Aurelius, both a Roman Emperor and a Stoic philosopher, penned this succinct yet powerful reminder in his *Meditations*. He advocated for authentic, principled living over hollow debate. This quote underscores the Stoic conviction that moral philosophy must be reflected in daily conduct rather than remain an intellectual exercise. For Marcus, the path to virtue was defined by action—taking purposeful steps to embody the qualities one values.

In a broader philosophical context, the challenge to "be" rather than merely discuss extends beyond Stoicism and resonates with modern teachings in psychology and ethics. It speaks to the concept of integrity—the alignment of one's values with one's behaviors. Likewise, psychologists often note that genuine leadership relies on consistency; when actions diverge from professed values, trust erodes. Whether we look at current research on character development or ancient wisdom, the conclusion is the same: living out one's beliefs cements them into reality.

When applied to parenting, the stakes become even more significant. Children absorb a great deal through observation and often emulate the behavior they witness. If parents preach virtues like honesty, discipline, and kindness but fail to uphold those qualities themselves, the lesson rings hollow. By leading through example, parents demonstrate how Stoic virtues and self-control translate into everyday decisions. In turn, children internalize not just the words but the lived demonstration of those principles—building a foundation of character that will guide them well beyond childhood.

Why Leading by Example Matters
Mirroring: Children Learn Through Observation

Leading by example is a profound concept that transcends mere guidance; it embodies the essence of influence through action. At the heart of this philosophy lies the understanding that human beings, particularly children, are inherently observant creatures. Their learning is not merely a product of verbal instruction but rather a complex interplay of imitation and internalization.

When we consider the mechanism of learning, it becomes evident that children are more attuned to the behaviors they witness than to the words they hear. Psychological studies reinforce this observation, highlighting that actions often speak louder than words. When parents and caregivers navigate the tumultuous waters of stress with calm and poise, they unwittingly provide a blueprint for their children to emulate. This mirroring effect is an integral aspect of development, as children absorb not only the actions but also the emotional responses associated with those actions.

Contradictions in behavior—where words do not align with actions—serve only to sow seeds of confusion and distrust within the formative minds of children. Such discrepancies can lead to a dissonance that complicates their understanding of the world around them. When a parent espouses the virtues of patience yet reacts with frustration, they inadvertently teach the child that words are mutable, while actions are definitive. This incongruity can erode the foundation of trust, leaving children grappling with uncertainty about the values they are expected to uphold.

In contrast, modeling desired traits through consistent behavior simplifies the process of imparting wisdom. Children, through daily exposure to positive role models, begin to internalize these behaviors, gradually forming habits that align with the values they observe. This process is not limited to the home environment; it extends to schools, communities, and society at large. As children witness integrity, kindness, and resilience in their role models, these traits become ingrained in their psyche, shaping their character and guiding their interactions with others.

The philosophy of leading by example thus serves as a reminder of the profound impact of our actions. It is an invitation to reflect on the legacy we leave behind—through our behaviors, we write the narratives of others' lives. In a world rife with challenges, the call to lead by example resonates as a timeless principle, urging us to embody the change we wish to see in the next generation. Through this lens, we recognize that the greatest lessons are often learned in the silent exchanges of observation, where the heart and spirit of our actions illuminate the path for those who follow.

Building Trust and Respect

Building trust and respect within the parent-child relationship is a cornerstone of effective parenting. Authentic behavior is not merely a guideline; it is a profound necessity. When parents embody the values they teach, they cultivate an environment where respect flourishes. Hypocrisy, on the other hand, acts as a corrosive agent, eroding parental authority and credibility.

Children possess an innate ability to discern when actions do not align with words. This inconsistency breeds confusion and resentment, leading them to question the very guidance intended to support their moral and ethical development. When parents model the behaviors they advocate—whether it's honesty, kindness, or responsibility—they provide a living example of integrity. This authenticity invites children to internalize these values, making them more likely to adhere to the guidance offered.

Discipline, when administered in a context of consistency, feels just and fair rather than arbitrary. Children thrive in environments where they can predict the consequences of their actions based on the clear alignment of parental expectations and behaviors. This predictability fosters a sense of justice, allowing them to understand the rationale behind rules and consequences, rather than viewing them as mere impositions.

As trust deepens, children begin to perceive their parents as reliable sources of wisdom and support. They gain confidence in the belief that their parents genuinely embody the principles they advocate. This trust nurtures a sense of security that is essential for open dialogue. In a trusting environment, children feel safe to express their thoughts and feelings, fostering deeper connections that enrich the parent-child relationship.

Ultimately, the interplay of trust and respect creates a dynamic that empowers children to grow into principled individuals. When parents lead by example, they not only cultivate a harmonious household but also equip their children with the moral compass necessary for navigating the complexities of life. In this way, the journey of parenting transforms into a shared exploration of values, reinforcing the bond between parent and child while shaping the future generation.

The Power of Embodied Virtues

The Power of Embodied Virtues in parenting is a profound concept that invites us to consider the daily choices we make and the virtues we embody. Stoicism teaches us that courage, wisdom, justice, and temperance are not mere ideals to be admired from a distance; they are practices to be lived. When parents actively embody these virtues, they do more than just teach; they transform. The daily demonstration of these principles creates a nurturing environment where children can thrive.

Imagine a parent who approaches each challenge with courage, facing fears and uncertainties head-on. This courageous demeanor cultivates a sense of security in children, assuring them that it is acceptable to confront their own fears. Wisdom, when practiced by a parent, manifests in thoughtful decisions and measured responses, helping children understand the importance of reflection and discernment in their own lives. Justice ensures that fairness and empathy are paramount in family interactions, teaching children to value equity and compassion. Temperance, particularly in moments of stress, illustrates self-restraint, showing young minds that even amidst turmoil, calmness and control can prevail.

These embodied virtues create a ripple effect. Children, observing their parents in action, begin to internalize these behaviors. A parent who demonstrates patience, even under duress, sends a powerful message: self-restraint is not only possible but beneficial. Over time, this modeling becomes a child's internal script, guiding them through life's inevitable ups and downs. They learn that challenges can be met with courage and that wisdom often comes from quiet contemplation.

This principle finds resonance in modern social learning theory, which underscores the significance of lived examples. Children are keen observers, absorbing lessons not just from words but from actions. When they see their parents navigating life's complexities with grace and virtue, they are more likely to adopt similar behaviors. The essence of learning in this context transcends mere instruction; it becomes a holistic experience rooted in observation and imitation.

Thus, the embodiment of virtues in parenting is not just an ethical choice; it is a strategic one. It fosters resilient, empathetic, and balanced individuals. The act of living these virtues daily becomes a powerful tool for shaping the next generation, ensuring that the values of courage, wisdom, justice, and temperance are not only inherited but also deeply ingrained. In a world where chaos often reigns, the steady hand of parents embodying these virtues can illuminate a path toward a brighter, more compassionate future for their children.

Boosting Your Own Growth

Boosting your own growth as a parent transcends mere responsibility; it becomes a profound journey of self-discovery and transformation. The act of striving to set a good example compels parents to refine their habits and attitudes, leading to an introspective examination of their own lives. In this context, the awareness that "little eyes" are watching serves as a potent motivator for personal improvement. Parents become acutely aware that their choices—whether in healthy eating, emotional regulation, or conflict resolution—are not just individual decisions but lessons being imparted to their children.

This dynamic aligns closely with the Stoic philosophy of continuous self-betterment. Stoicism emphasizes the importance of virtue and self-control, urging individuals to live in accordance with their values. As parents embrace this philosophy, they recognize that their growth is not a solitary endeavor but a shared journey with their children. By embodying the principles they wish to instill, parents create an environment where both they and their children can flourish.

Moreover, parenting can ignite a renewed sense of purpose. When parents actively live their values—nurturing kindness, resilience, and integrity—they not only teach these qualities but also reinforce their own commitment to them. This alignment of personal values with parenting responsibilities fosters a sense of fulfillment that transcends the challenges of day-to-day life.

As this mutual growth occurs, a unified family culture emerges, characterized by a collective striving for excellence. Parents and children alike learn that growth is not merely an individual pursuit; it is a shared journey that strengthens familial bonds. In nurturing this culture, families cultivate resilience, adaptability, and a commitment to lifelong learning, creating a legacy of excellence that echoes through generations.

Ultimately, the act of boosting your own growth as a parent is an invitation to embrace the transformative power of love and responsibility. By recognizing the impact of their actions, parents can inspire not only their children but themselves, fostering an environment where growth is celebrated and achieved together.

Long-Term Family Culture

The concept of long-term family culture resonates profoundly within the intricate tapestry of human experience, revealing the interplay between individual development and collective legacy. In a household where virtues such as discipline, empathy, and honesty are not merely taught but consistently modeled, an environment is cultivated that transcends the immediate interactions of daily life. This nurturing space becomes a crucible for character formation, shaping the very essence of children who inhabit it.

As children observe their parents and elders embodying these virtues, they internalize these behaviors, learning not just to mimic but to understand the underlying significance of such principles. The act of modeling virtues serves as a silent yet powerful pedagogy; it instills in them a sense of accountability that is essential for personal growth. In this dynamic, the child becomes a mirror, reflecting back the values they witness, and in turn, they learn to hold themselves accountable to those same standards. This reflective process is crucial, as it fosters an intrinsic motivation to embody the virtues they have seen in action.

The notion of a "virtuous cycle" emerges from this modeling, where each generation inherits the moral architecture established by the previous one. This cyclical transmission of values creates a familial legacy that is resilient and principled, reinforcing the idea that virtues are not static but rather dynamic elements that evolve through practice and commitment. Each act of kindness, discipline, or honesty becomes a building block, fortifying the foundation upon which future generations can stand.

Moreover, leading by example is not merely a guideline for parenting; it is a profound philosophical assertion regarding the nature of influence and responsibility within familial structures. It posits that the most effective way to impart values is through lived experience rather than through mere instruction. In this light, the family becomes a microcosm of society itself, illustrating how the cultivation of virtues within the intimate sphere can resonate outward, influencing broader social norms and expectations.

Ultimately, the long-term family culture is not just about raising children; it is about nurturing a legacy of virtue that can withstand the tests of time. It is an invitation to reflect on how our actions today shape the moral landscape of tomorrow, urging us to consider the weight of our responsibilities as guardians of these values. The challenge lies in recognizing that each moment, each interaction, is an opportunity to either reinforce or undermine the very culture we seek to cultivate, thus underscoring the importance of intentionality in our daily lives.

The Role of Discipline in Daily Life
Dispelling Myths About Discipline

Discipline is often misunderstood, misconstrued as a harsh measure of punishment rather than a framework for self-regulation and consistent routines. This misconception obscures the true essence of discipline, which is fundamentally about cultivating the ability to make wise choices. As Ryan Holiday eloquently states, "Discipline is the bridge between goals and accomplishment." It is through this lens that we can appreciate discipline not as an imposition, but as a vital tool for personal growth and freedom.

Stoic philosophy teaches us that true discipline is rooted in the understanding that our choices shape our lives. It encourages us to respond to challenges with wisdom rather than fear-driven obedience. This approach fosters an environment where individuals, especially children, learn to govern their own impulses rather than simply adhering to arbitrary rules. When discipline is exercised with empathy and respect, it nurtures a sense of agency and responsibility, guiding children toward their own growth rather than stifling their spirit.

Moreover, discipline devoid of rationale can lead to rebellion or secrecy. When rules are imposed without explanation, they can feel oppressive rather than constructive. Children subjected to such discipline may feel trapped, leading them to act out in ways that undermine the very structure intended to guide them. In contrast, healthy discipline aligns with the principles of empathy and respect, creating a foundation where children can thrive. It empowers them to understand the reasons behind their actions, fostering a sense of inner freedom that comes from self-regulation rather than external control.

In this light, discipline becomes not only a practice but a philosophy—one that encourages reflection, growth, and the development of character. By embracing discipline as a guiding force rather than a punitive measure, we can cultivate a culture of resilience and wisdom, allowing individuals to navigate life's complexities with confidence and integrity.

Setting Personal Standards First

Setting personal standards first serves as a profound testament to the principle of integrity in parenting. Children, in their formative years, possess an acute sensitivity to the discrepancies between words and actions. They observe their parents not merely as caregivers but as living embodiments of values and rules. When parents impose limitations, such as restricting screen time or advocating for a neat household, their own adherence to these standards becomes a cornerstone of credibility.

In this delicate dance of influence, parents who exemplify their personal commitments—be it punctuality, honesty, or respect—instill an intrinsic sense of responsibility within their children. This is not merely a matter of enforcing rules; it is an invitation for children to internalize these virtues as they witness their parents embodying them. The act of demonstrating commitment does not only speak to the children's minds but resonates within their hearts, fostering an environment where accountability becomes a shared family ethos.

Furthermore, establishing clear and consistent routines—be it morning rituals or designated study hours—provides a framework that illustrates discipline in action. Such routines are not mere schedules; they are rituals of intention, shaping the fabric of daily life and imbuing it with purpose. In observing these practices, children learn that structure and discipline are not burdens but rather guiding principles that allow for personal growth and achievement.

In essence, when parents prioritize their own standards and actively engage in the practices they advocate, they cultivate an atmosphere of mutual respect and shared values. This philosophical approach transcends mere behavioral compliance; it nurtures a deeper understanding of responsibility, one that children can carry forward into their own lives as they navigate the complexities of the world.

Aligning Family Rules with Core Values

The Story of Cincinnatus and the Plow

Cincinnatus, an ancient Roman farmer, was called to be a dictator during a tough time. He quickly led Rome to victory and brought back peace. Instead of holding onto power, he chose to go back to his farm, showing a remarkable sense of humility and duty. His story highlights living a life guided by virtue rather than ambition or ego. For parents, Cincinnatus's decision to return to farming reminds us that true leadership is about humble service—an important part of Stoic virtue. We have authority in our homes, but it's crucial to approach it without ego, viewing parenting as a way to serve our family rather than seeking power. By practicing self-restraint, we can set rules and discipline with kindness, allowing our children the freedom to grow. We honor them through our actions: by leading by example, taking our responsibilities seriously, and understanding that "control" isn't the same as genuine influence. This mindset helps us be authentic stewards; once we've done our part, we allow our children to thrive, just as Cincinnatus returned to his fields.

In the intricate tapestry of family life, the alignment of rules with core values emerges as a profound philosophical endeavor. Rules, when merely imposed, can become shackles; however, when they resonate with virtues such as kindness, fairness, and perseverance, they morph into beacons of meaning and purpose. It is through the lens of these virtues that we can cultivate an environment where rules are not merely constraints but rather guiding principles that illuminate the path of familial interactions.

The essence of explaining the "why" behind rules cannot be overstated. In this act of elucidation, parents impart a sense of purpose that transcends mere compliance. Children, when they grasp the rationale behind the rules, begin to see them not as arbitrary restrictions but as essential components of a larger ethical framework. This understanding fosters a sense of agency, empowering children to internalize these values and apply them in their everyday lives.

A family culture steeped in shared values acts as a unifying force, drawing each member into a collective vision. This shared ethos creates a sanctuary where individual differences are celebrated, yet everyone is anchored to a common purpose. It is within this culture that the rules take on a deeper significance, as they are collectively seen as the embodiment of the shared virtues that bind the family together.

Inviting children to participate in the formulation of certain guidelines is an act that nurtures their sense of ownership and responsibility. When children feel that their voices are heard and their perspectives valued, they are more likely to embrace the rules as their own. This collaborative approach shifts the dynamics of discipline from a top-down enforcement to a shared commitment, where each family member feels an intrinsic motivation to uphold the agreed-upon values.

Thus, the alignment of family rules with core values transforms the landscape of familial discipline. It fosters an atmosphere where rules are not perceived as punitive measures but as expressions of love, respect, and a shared journey toward moral development. In this harmonious alignment, family life flourishes, cultivating not only respectful individuals but also a cohesive unit that embodies the very virtues it espouses.

Consistency as a Key Factor

Consistency serves as a cornerstone for the healthy development of children, establishing a framework within which they can explore their world with confidence. Children, by nature, are sensitive to their environments; they thrive on predictability, which helps them make sense of the complexities around them. When parents set and maintain consistent boundaries, they provide a sense of security that reduces confusion and anxiety. This security is essential for children to develop a strong sense of self and the ability to navigate social interactions.

Inconsistency, on the other hand, erodes the foundation of parental authority. When rules are enforced one day and disregarded the next, children become confused about expectations and consequences. This inconsistency not only diminishes the respect children hold for parental guidance but also impedes their understanding of right and wrong. The Stoics understood the importance of steadfastness; they believed that once a principle is recognized as virtuous, it must be upheld with unwavering commitment. This philosophy is particularly relevant in parenting, where the steadfast application of values and rules fosters an environment of reliability.

Moreover, when parents engage in the consistent correction of misbehavior—delivered calmly and constructively—they are not merely disciplining; they are actively facilitating the internalization of positive habits. Children learn through repetition and reinforcement, and consistent guidance allows them to assimilate the lessons of morality and ethics into their own value systems. As they witness their parents embodying these principles, they are inspired to adopt similar behaviors, cultivating a character grounded in virtue.

Over time, the practice of consistency builds trust. Children come to rely on their parents as stable figures who offer clear guidance amidst the chaos of life. This trust is crucial for creating a stable environment conducive to learning. In such an environment, children feel safe to take risks, make mistakes, and ultimately grow. They are more willing to engage with new ideas and challenges when they know that their foundational support is unshakable.

The importance of consistency in parenting cannot be overstated. It is not merely a method of discipline; it is a profound commitment to fostering a nurturing, predictable space where children can flourish. By embodying the principles of steadfastness and reliability, parents can guide their children toward becoming well-adjusted individuals capable of navigating the complexities of life with confidence and integrity.

Positive Reinforcement and Encouragement

In the realm of child development and education, the interplay of positive reinforcement and encouragement serves as a crucial philosophical inquiry into the nature of discipline. Discipline, often perceived as a rigid mechanism for enforcing rules, finds its true efficacy when harmonized with the acknowledgment of constructive behavior. This duality invites us to reflect on the essence of growth and the human experience itself.

Recognizing incremental improvements becomes a testament to the journey of learning, akin to a Stoic perspective that values progress over perfection. Each small success serves as a beacon of motivation, urging children to persist in their endeavors. It is through this lens that we celebrate effort, self-control, and resilience—qualities that resonate deeply with Stoic virtues. The Stoics teach that virtue is found not in the outcome but in the consistent practice of these fundamental traits.

Positive reinforcement emerges as a powerful tool in nurturing a child's belief in their capacity for self-regulation. When adults validate a child's efforts, they not only affirm the value of hard work but also cultivate an internal locus of control. This psychological empowerment is essential; it fosters confidence and instills a readiness to confront challenges, echoing the Stoic ideal of facing adversity with fortitude.

Moreover, the synthesis of structure and affirmation creates an environment conducive to growth. Structure provides the necessary boundaries within which children can explore and experiment, while affirmation nurtures their spirit, encouraging them to stretch beyond their comfort zones. This balance reflects a philosophical understanding of human potential—each individual thrives not solely through external discipline but through the internal motivation derived from recognition and support.

In essence, the philosophical exploration of positive reinforcement and encouragement reveals a deeper truth about human development. It illustrates that the path to maturity is not marked merely by the avoidance of missteps but rather by the celebration of efforts, resilience, and the continuous pursuit of virtue. Each act of encouragement becomes a philosophical act, reinforcing the belief that growth is a shared journey, one that can be nurtured through mindful recognition and support.

Self-Control and Emotional Regulation

The Stoic Perspective on Emotions

Stoicism teaches us that emotions are not inherently negative; they are a natural part of our human experience. "We suffer more often in imagination than in reality," said Seneca, highlighting the need for reason to guide our emotional responses. In the realm of parenting, where emotions run high—love, pride, frustration, and worry—it becomes vital to cultivate self-control and emotional regulation. By embracing our emotions without letting them dictate our actions, we can model a balanced approach for our children.

When parents harness their emotions productively, they create an environment where healthy expression is encouraged rather than stifled. This practice not only benefits the parents but also serves as a powerful lesson for children. By demonstrating the distinction between feeling an emotion and being ruled by it, parents teach their children the value of emotional intelligence. This balanced outlook aligns seamlessly with modern psychology, which underscores the importance of recognizing and managing our feelings.

In this light, the Stoic perspective becomes not merely a philosophical doctrine but a practical guide for nurturing resilient, emotionally aware children. This approach fosters an atmosphere where emotions are acknowledged, understood, and ultimately transformed into opportunities for growth and connection. Thus, embracing the Stoic wisdom on emotions allows parents to cultivate a profound legacy of emotional resilience and intelligence in their offspring, preparing them to navigate the complexities of life with grace and reason.

Recognizing Your Triggers

Recognizing one's triggers serves as a profound journey into the depths of self-awareness, an essential tenet of philosophical inquiry. In the vast landscape of human experience, certain stimuli elicit visceral reactions—anger, impatience, anxiety—that often seem to arise unbidden. To engage in the act of self-control, one must first embark on the path of identification, illuminating those personal hot buttons that disrupt the equilibrium of the mind.

This awareness is not merely an academic exercise; it is an invitation to cultivate strategies for maintaining composure amidst turmoil. Breathing exercises and mental reframing are tools that empower the individual, allowing a shift from reaction to reflection. Such practices serve as a sanctuary in the chaotic storm of emotions, enabling one to respond with intentionality rather than impulse.

As guardians of the next generation, parents wield a unique influence in this realm. By consistently navigating their triggers with grace, they create an environment where children feel secure and understood. This dynamic fosters a profound sense of safety, even in moments of correction. The child learns that while behavior may be addressed, the love and acceptance remain steadfast, a philosophical cornerstone of nurturing relationships.

Moreover, the act of apologizing when one falters is an embodiment of humility and authenticity. This admission of imperfection not only models vulnerability for children but also teaches them that growth lies within the embrace of our shortcomings. It reinforces the idea that to err is human, and to rectify is divine—a timeless lesson that nurtures empathy and understanding.

In this cycle of recognition, response, and reflection, parents gradually build resilience. The habitual reactions that once dictated their interactions begin to dissolve, replaced by a measured approach that fosters connection rather than disconnection. Over time, the negative spirals of reaction give way to a tapestry of constructive responses, weaving a narrative that elevates both parent and child.

Thus, recognizing triggers transcends mere self-control; it becomes a philosophical practice that enriches the soul, nurtures relationships, and fosters a legacy of understanding and empathy. In this pursuit, both parent and child embark on a journey toward a more harmonious existence, grounded in the recognition of their shared humanity.

Techniques for Maintaining Composure

In the quest for maintaining composure, it becomes essential to adopt techniques that anchor us in the present, allowing for clarity amidst chaos. The "Five-Second Rule" stands as a powerful tool, inviting us to pause before reacting in moments of tension. This brief interlude, a mere count of five, serves not only to temper our immediate impulses but also to grant us the space to consider our response thoughtfully. In a world that often rewards rapid reactions, this practice encourages us to value reflection over reflex.

Reframing our perspective is equally crucial. When faced with adversity, it is all too easy to inflate the urgency of a situation, letting our minds spiral into a state of heightened anxiety. By asking ourselves whether the issue at hand truly warrants such urgency, we can often deflate its perceived importance. This shift in mindset fosters a sense of control, allowing us to navigate challenges with a steadier hand and a clearer vision.

Our bodies, too, communicate vital information that can aid in maintaining composure. Recognizing physical cues—such as a racing heart or tense muscles—acts as a reminder to slow down. These signals are not mere indicators of stress; they are invitations to breathe, to ground ourselves, and to reclaim our composure. By acknowledging these bodily responses, we empower ourselves to respond rather than react, reinforcing our sense of agency in turbulent moments.

In this journey of composure, the use of mantras or key phrases can serve as a mental anchor. A simple phrase like "Calm leads, anger misleads" encapsulates profound wisdom. Such affirmations provide immediate clarity, redirecting our thoughts when faced with emotional turbulence. They remind us of the virtues of calmness and the pitfalls of allowing anger to dictate our actions, reinforcing the crucial distinction between being proactive and reactive.

Finally, post-event decompression is an essential practice in the art of maintaining composure. Engaging in a brief walk or practicing mindful breathing after a stressful encounter allows us to reset our minds and bodies. This intentional act of self-care not only aids in recovery but also equips us with the resilience to face future challenges. Embracing these moments of reflection fosters a deeper understanding of our responses, enabling us to emerge from stressful situations with greater poise and insight.

Incorporating these techniques into our daily lives can transform how we engage with the world around us. By committing to pause, reflect, and recalibrate, we cultivate an inner strength that transcends the chaos, allowing us to navigate life's complexities with grace and wisdom.

Modeling Self-Control for Children

Modeling self-control for children is not merely an act of discipline; it is a profound gift that shapes their understanding of emotional resilience and conflict resolution. In every instance of provocation or setback, children observe their parents, absorbing not just the actions but the underlying philosophies that guide those actions. When parents respond to challenges with respect and measured behavior, they provide a living template for their children, one that communicates that emotional outbursts are neither the norm nor an effective means of navigating life's inevitable frustrations.

Consider the power of involvement in open conversations about emotions. When a parent shares, "I felt upset, but I took a breath and thought it through," they are not just recounting an experience; they are imparting wisdom. This simple act of reflection teaches children emotional literacy, enabling them to recognize and articulate their feelings. It introduces them to a spectrum of emotions and the importance of processing them in a constructive manner. This transparency fosters a safe space where children can explore their feelings without fear of judgment, encouraging them to develop responsible coping mechanisms.

Furthermore, calm parental leadership nurtures an environment of mutual respect and understanding. This is crucial in a world where quick reactions often overshadow thoughtful responses. When children witness their parents navigating emotional turmoil with grace and composure, they learn that it is possible to face adversity without succumbing to destructive impulses. They come to understand that true strength lies not in the immediate expression of frustration but in the ability to pause, assess, and respond thoughtfully.

In essence, the practice of modeling self-control cultivates a legacy of emotional intelligence. As children learn to manage their own responses, they become equipped to handle the complexities of relationships and life challenges. They learn that respect is foundational to any interaction, and that understanding oneself is the first step toward understanding others. In this way, parents do not just teach self-control; they foster a culture of empathy and resilience that will benefit their children throughout their lives. The impact of such modeling reaches far beyond the immediate family, extending into the community, as children grow to become thoughtful, respectful individuals capable of navigating the world with integrity and understanding.

Long-Term Benefits of Self-Control

Children who master self-regulation not only enhance their own lives but also cultivate an environment that benefits everyone around them. By learning patience, emotional resilience, and respect for others, they develop essential skills that will serve them well in friendships, academic pursuits, and, ultimately, their careers. These traits are invaluable; they foster strong connections with peers, enabling children to navigate the complexities of social interactions with grace and understanding.

Moreover, when parents model and encourage self-control, they experience a profound boost in self-esteem. Responding thoughtfully rather than reacting impulsively allows parents to handle challenges with poise, reinforcing a sense of competence and confidence. This shift in behavior significantly reduces household tensions, transforming potential conflicts into opportunities for constructive communication. Families that embrace self-control create a sanctuary of support and understanding, where each member feels valued and heard.

The long-term benefits of self-control extend far beyond individual achievements. They lay the foundation for a virtuous, harmonious family life. As children grow into adults, the lessons learned in self-regulation will guide them in making ethical decisions and maintaining healthy relationships. In a world that often feels chaotic and unpredictable, fostering self-control is not just beneficial; it is essential for nurturing future generations capable of contributing positively to society. Investing in self-control today means reaping the rewards of resilient, respectful, and responsible individuals tomorrow.

Teaching Virtue in Small Moments
Everyday Opportunities for Virtue

Virtues like honesty and kindness do not necessitate grand gestures or monumental events; they thrive in the small, often overlooked moments of daily life. It is within these seemingly mundane interactions—waiting patiently in line, tidying up after oneself, or engaging in polite conversation—that the seeds of virtue are sown. These moments serve as prime teaching opportunities, allowing us to reinforce that virtue is fundamentally a habit rather than a rare display of moral excellence.

As Aristotle wisely stated, "We are what we repeatedly do. Excellence, then, is not an act, but a habit." This quote encapsulates the essence of virtue as a practice woven into the fabric of everyday existence. When children witness and practice small acts of virtue, they begin to internalize the belief that their character is revealed not in extraordinary circumstances, but in the ordinary. Each time they choose patience over impatience, or kindness over indifference, they are not just performing a good deed; they are cultivating a disposition that will guide their choices throughout life.

These cumulative lessons have a profound impact on a child's long-term ethical framework. By consistently engaging in and observing virtuous behavior in everyday situations, children learn that virtue is not an isolated event, but a continuous journey. They come to understand that their actions, however small, contribute to the greater tapestry of their character. In this way, the cultivation of virtue becomes a powerful, ongoing process, shaping not only who they are but also how they relate to the world around them. Emphasizing the importance of small moments in teaching virtue lays the groundwork for a future where ethical principles are not just understood, but lived fully and authentically.

Turning Mistakes into Lessons

In the tapestry of human experience, mistakes emerge not as blemishes but as integral threads that weave the fabric of wisdom. When children or parents stumble, the inclination to retreat into shame is a natural one, yet it is precisely in these moments of misstep that profound opportunities for reflection and adjustment arise. Rather than casting a shadow over the individual, these errors illuminate the path toward a deeper understanding of oneself and one's values.

Consider how a different choice, perhaps one rooted in honesty or patience, could have yielded a more harmonious outcome. Such reflections do not serve to chastise but to enlighten, inviting individuals to recognize the myriad possibilities that lie before them. It is within this contemplation that the seeds of personal growth are sown, allowing one to cultivate a richer, more nuanced perspective on life's challenges.

Adopting a Stoic approach, we find solace in the notion that failures are not the end of the journey but rather stepping stones toward greater wisdom. The Stoics teach us that the fear of trying often stems from an inflated view of failure. By reframing our perception, we can embrace mistakes as necessary components of a meaningful existence, liberating ourselves from the shackles of apprehension. In doing so, we empower ourselves and those around us to venture forth with courage and curiosity.

Encouraging open dialogue about what went awry transforms the narrative surrounding failure. It becomes a shared exploration rather than an isolated experience steeped in shame. This discourse allows individuals to voice their thoughts and feelings, fostering an environment where mistakes are not hidden but discussed openly. Such transparency cultivates trust and understanding, reinforcing the idea that everyone is a work in progress, perpetually learning and evolving.

Over time, this practice nurtures a culture where mistakes are acknowledged as essential milestones along the journey of growth. In this environment, the emphasis shifts from avoiding errors to embracing them as vital lessons. As individuals engage with their missteps, they develop resilience and adaptability, essential traits for navigating the complexities of life. In this way, mistakes become not only acceptable but celebrated as catalysts for insight and transformation.

Family Discussions on Values

Family discussions on values serve as a crucible for the moral fabric that binds individuals together. When families gather, perhaps around the dinner table, to engage in dialogues about fundamental virtues such as respect, courage, and kindness, they are not merely exchanging pleasantries; they are actively embedding these ideals into the very essence of their relationships. Such conversations transform abstract concepts into tangible commitments that resonate within the hearts and minds of family members.

In these discussions, it is essential to share personal experiences that reveal the struggle to embody these virtues. For instance, when one grapples with the challenge of demonstrating kindness in a moment of frustration, it becomes an opportunity for reflection and growth. This admission of vulnerability highlights the reality that virtue is not a fixed trait but rather a continuous journey of learning and self-improvement. By acknowledging our imperfections, we create an atmosphere of authenticity, inviting others to explore their own challenges in embodying these ideals.

Encouraging children to articulate their understanding of virtues in their own words fosters deeper engagement. This exercise not only empowers them but also allows for a richer dialogue that can reveal diverse interpretations and insights. When children define respect, courage, and kindness through their unique lenses, they begin to take ownership of these values, transforming them from mere words into guiding principles that influence their actions.

Moreover, discussing real-life or fictional scenarios provides a fertile ground for examining the complexities of moral choices. Posing questions such as, "What would be the virtuous choice here?" invites critical thinking and moral reasoning. It challenges family members to dissect situations, consider various perspectives, and deliberate on the implications of their choices. Through these conversations, the family not only cultivates an understanding of virtue but also prepares to navigate the moral dilemmas that life inevitably presents.

As these discussions become normalized within the family dynamic, they weave virtue into the everyday language and interactions of its members. The ideals of respect, courage, and kindness cease to be abstract concepts; they evolve into vital components of the familial identity. In this way, the home becomes a sanctuary of values, a place where individuals are nurtured not just in knowledge, but in character. Ultimately, it is through this collective pursuit of virtue that families can aspire to become beacons of moral clarity in an often chaotic world.

Acknowledging Effort and Progress

In a world increasingly focused on outcomes, it is essential to shift our perspective toward the virtues that foster genuine growth in children. Acknowledging effort and progress transcends mere recognition of achievements; it cultivates a deeper understanding of the moral fabric that weaves through the tapestry of human experience. When we praise children for their restraint, kindness, or diligence, we are not simply applauding what they have done but rather affirming the character they are developing. This emphasis on virtue over result aligns seamlessly with both Stoic philosophy and contemporary psychological insights.

Consider the value of validating a child's effort to remain truthful or calm under pressure. Such moments are not trivial; they represent the struggles and victories of self-mastery. By recognizing those instances, we illuminate the path to resilience and integrity, encouraging children to embrace their internal struggles as part of their growth. When a child faces frustration yet manages to take a deep breath, celebrating that small victory reinforces a profound lesson: that the journey toward virtue is as important, if not more so, than the destination.

This targeted encouragement fosters an environment where children begin to internalize the notion that virtuous behavior is intrinsically fulfilling. They learn that the act of exercising restraint or demonstrating kindness is not merely a means to an end but an end in itself. As they experience the positive feedback associated with their efforts, they cultivate a sense of pride in their character, which is far more enduring than the fleeting satisfaction of external rewards.

In time, children come to associate virtuous behavior with their own sense of self-worth. They realize that living in accordance with their values provides a deeper, more meaningful fulfillment than any accolade could offer. This alignment with Stoic principles, which advocate for the cultivation of virtue as the highest good, helps children navigate the complexities of life with a steady heart and a clear mind.

Ultimately, by recognizing and celebrating effort and progress, we equip the next generation with the tools they need to thrive. We instill in them a profound understanding that true fulfillment stems from their character, not just their accomplishments. This philosophical approach not only nurtures personal growth but also lays the groundwork for a more compassionate and resilient society.

Leading with Empathy

Leading with empathy is not just a practice; it is the foundation of effective parenting and a cornerstone of Stoic philosophy. It allows us to recognize and validate our child's feelings while maintaining the necessary boundaries that ensure their growth and safety. By acknowledging their perspective, we demonstrate that self-control does not diminish compassion; instead, it enhances our ability to connect meaningfully.

Empathetic leadership cultivates an environment of mutual respect and cooperation, forging a resilient parent-child bond that can withstand the trials of life. When we model empathy, we impart vital lessons to our children about honoring their own emotions and understanding those of others. As the philosopher Marcus Aurelius wisely stated, "When you wake up in the morning, tell yourself: The people I deal with today will be meddling, ungrateful, arrogant, dishonest, jealous, and surly." This reminder encourages us to respond with empathy rather than frustration, reinforcing the notion that compassion is the most powerful tool we possess in nurturing our relationships. In this way, leading with empathy not only enriches our parenting journey but also shapes our children into emotionally intelligent individuals who value connection and understanding in their own lives.

Sustaining Momentum Over Time
Consistency Amid Life's Changes

Families evolve—children grow, schedules shift, new challenges arise. In these moments of change, your commitment to lead by example becomes even more critical. Embracing the philosophy of Stoicism, we recognize that change is an inherent part of life. It is your steady presence during these transitions that offers the stability your family needs.

Regularly revisiting your guiding principles is essential. Are they still aligned with your family's current reality? This reflection is not merely an exercise; it is a necessity. As life evolves, your values and the principles you instill must remain relevant to the circumstances your family faces. By doing so, you ensure that your leadership adapts, staying effective in guiding your loved ones through the complexities of life.

Adaptation, however, must be carried out with integrity. When you adjust your approach, do so in a way that remains true to your core values. This consistency amidst change does not mean rigidly adhering to outdated practices; instead, it means responding thoughtfully and purposefully to new situations while maintaining your commitment to your family's well-being.

Your ability to navigate these transitions with a steady hand reinforces your family's trust in your leadership. They will look to you not only for direction but also for reassurance that, despite the changes, the foundation of your family remains strong. By embodying these principles, you foster an environment where growth is not only possible but celebrated, ensuring that your family thrives through every chapter of their lives.

Revisiting and Renewing Your Own Virtues

Revisiting and renewing your own virtues is essential for personal growth, especially as a parent. In the relentless flow of everyday responsibilities, it is all too easy to lose sight of our own development. The virtues we wish to instill in our children are often the very qualities we must consciously embody ourselves. This duality of role—both a guide and a learner—requires us to take a step back and assess our progress.

Engaging in periodic reflection is not merely a luxury but a necessity. By asking ourselves whether we embody the virtues we wish to pass on, we confront a profound philosophical inquiry: What does it mean to live a virtuous life? This introspection can reveal the discrepancies between our ideals and our actions, prompting us to bridge that gap.

Seeking feedback from partners or friends serves as a crucial mechanism for self-awareness. An outside perspective can illuminate blind spots we may not recognize in our self-assessment. This act of vulnerability—inviting others to critique our behavior and principles—can be transformative. It opens the door to growth, showing us how our virtues are perceived in the world beyond our immediate circle.

Moreover, the commitment to self-improvement should be viewed as a continuous journey, not a destination. Embracing our mistakes as integral to this process allows us to cultivate resilience. Each misstep can be a lesson, shaping our character and reinforcing the very virtues we aspire to embody. This mindset not only enriches our own lives but also sets a powerful example for our children. By demonstrating that growth is a lifelong pursuit, we encourage them to adopt a similar ethos.

Ultimately, the refinement of our virtues is a reciprocal process, benefiting both ourselves and our children. As we strive to model lifelong learning, we create an environment where growth and self-examination are valued. In this shared journey, we not only elevate our own character but also nurture the next generation to become thoughtful, compassionate individuals who understand the importance of revisiting and renewing their own virtues as they navigate their paths in life.

Encouraging Self-Reliance in Children

Encouraging self-reliance in children is essential for their development into responsible and independent adults. As children grow, it is important to gradually transfer more responsibility to them. This approach allows them to practice discipline and self-control in a safe environment. By assigning age-appropriate tasks, parents can help children learn to manage their time and resources effectively.

Encouraging children to resolve minor conflicts independently fosters problem-solving skills. When they face disagreements or challenges, guiding them to think critically about possible solutions empowers them to take ownership of their actions. This not only builds their confidence but also reduces reliance on parental intervention for every issue.

Celebrating each step toward autonomy is a vital part of this process. Acknowledging their efforts, no matter how small, reinforces the idea that self-discipline is a personal journey. It is important to convey that discipline should come from within rather than being imposed by others. This perspective allows children to develop intrinsic motivation.

Leading by example is crucial in this journey. When children observe their parents handling challenges with responsibility and integrity, they learn to emulate those behaviors. Witnessing their own growth and ability to tackle difficulties affirms their capabilities and reinforces the lessons taught.

Over time, the cumulative effect of these practices prepares children to become well-equipped young adults. They embody the virtues of responsibility, resilience, and self-reliance, reflecting the values modeled throughout their upbringing. This foundation not only benefits them personally but also contributes positively to their interactions with others and their overall success in life.

Guarding Against Burnout

Upholding high standards in any endeavor is a noble pursuit, yet it often carries with it the weight of exhaustion. The relentless drive for excellence can, at times, obscure the vital necessity of self-care and pause. In the wisdom of Stoicism, we find a call for prudence—a measured approach to our ambitions. It is essential to recognize our limits, for to overextend ourselves is to invite the very fatigue we seek to evade.

In the practice of leadership, the act of seeking help or delegating tasks becomes an exercise in humility and wisdom, particularly when imparting these lessons to the younger generation. Teaching children the importance of balance is not merely about managing workloads; it is about cultivating a mindset that values well-being alongside achievement. In this way, we equip them with the tools to navigate their own journeys without succumbing to the pressures that often accompany high expectations.

Moreover, the preservation of one's mental and emotional health is paramount in sustaining effective leadership. A leader who neglects their own needs risks becoming a vessel of discontent, unable to inspire or uplift others. Healthy boundaries serve as a protective barrier against the encroachment of resentment, which can silently erode the integrity of one's example.

Self-awareness, then, becomes an indispensable ally in this quest for balance. It calls for an ongoing dialogue with oneself, a reflection on one's state of being that allows for the recalibration of energy and focus. In honoring our own well-being, we affirm our commitment to our roles, ensuring that we lead not from a place of depletion but from a reservoir of vitality and purpose. Thus, nurturing oneself is not an indulgence; it is a profound act of responsibility that enhances our capacity to guide others with integrity and passion.

Celebrating Milestones and Growth

Celebrating milestones and growth is essential in recognizing the journey that shapes not only individual lives but the collective experience of a family. Each small victory, each hurdle overcome, serves as a testament to resilience and shared strength. This acknowledgment is not merely a celebration of achievements but a moment to reflect on the values that guided the family through trials—the Stoic virtues of wisdom, courage, justice, and temperance.

Sharing stories of successes, whether big or small, allows family members to see the interconnectedness of their experiences. These narratives become a tapestry of support and understanding, reinforcing the idea that each struggle faced was not faced alone. Through these reflections, the family cultivates a deeper bond, a shared resolve that fortifies them against future challenges. The act of reminiscing about how Stoic principles have influenced decisions during tough times highlights the importance of these virtues in navigating life's complexities.

As appreciation for growth solidifies into new habits, virtuous conduct becomes an intrinsic part of daily life. The practice of recognizing and celebrating progress transforms these values from mere concepts into lived experiences. They no longer feel like burdensome expectations but rather natural inclinations—an organic expression of character that is both rewarding and fulfilling.

In this light, leading by example weaves a narrative that transcends time, embedding these principles into the family's legacy. Each member becomes a custodian of the virtues learned, passing them down through generations. This narrative is not static; it evolves as new milestones are celebrated, new lessons are learned, and new stories are shared.

In conclusion, the journey of growth and celebration serves as a profound reminder of the transient yet impactful nature of life. Each milestone is a stepping stone that not only marks progress but also deepens the understanding of one's place within the greater tapestry of existence. It is through these moments of reflection and acknowledgment that we find meaning, purpose, and a sense of belonging. The legacy of this journey is not merely in the achievements themselves but in the virtues that guide us, the bonds that unite us, and the stories that will continue to inspire those who come after us. In embracing both the struggles and successes, we discover that life, in all its complexities, is a celebration of growth—a continuous unfolding of potential rooted in the wisdom of our shared experiences.

Key Takeaways (Chapter Cheat Sheet)

1. Children Mimic What They See

    ◦ Authentic behavior resonates more than verbal lectures, cementing values through everyday observation.
2. Discipline is About Self-Regulation, Not Punishment

    ◦ Stoic discipline guides a family's moral compass, emphasizing constructive habits and personal responsibility.
3. Self-Control Models Emotional Intelligence

    ◦ Demonstrating composure under stress teaches children to navigate their own feelings and conflicts wisely.
4. Small Moments Build Big Character

    ◦ Daily routines and minor decisions offer continual chances to embody honesty, patience, and empathy.
5. Consistency Fosters Family Culture

- Steadfast application of virtues—adapted over time—creates a lasting legacy of trust, respect, and growth.

Reflection Prompts

1. Journaling Exercise

    - Recall a recent situation where your actions didn't align with the virtues you want to model. What triggered the misalignment, and how might you respond differently next time?

2. Family Discussion

    - Ask each family member (children included) to share a moment when they noticed someone in the family modeling a particular virtue. How did that moment affect their perspective or behavior?

3. Action Step

    - Identify one virtue (e.g., patience or discipline) you'll consciously practice this week. Jot down at least one small way you can demonstrate it each day—then note the results.

Leading by example goes beyond mere words; it's a lifestyle of integrity, discipline, and heartfelt empathy. By living out Stoic principles, you create a powerful blueprint for your children to follow, equipping them with virtues that stand the test of time.

Four

Patience Is Power

"*How much better to heal than seek revenge from injury; vengeance consumes much time and it exposes the sore, whereas patience and moderation heal and close it.*"
— Seneca

Seneca, one of the most influential Roman Stoic philosophers, penned numerous letters and essays emphasizing the virtues of forbearance and composure. His reminder that patience heals more effectively than hostility reflects the Stoic conviction that a measured response to provocation yields far greater benefit than an impulsive reaction. Seneca perceived anger and revenge as wastes of energy—clouding our ability to make wise decisions and build strong relationships.

From a broader philosophical and psychological perspective, patience is more than simply "waiting." It is a proactive stance that demands self-control, empathy, and trust in the process of growth or resolution. Recent research in developmental psychology shows that children who witness patient behavior in their caregivers often develop higher levels of emotional regulation and resilience. Like Seneca, modern psychology underscores that a calm, deliberate approach to conflict resolution not only preserves mental well-being but also fosters deeper connections with others.

In the parenting sphere, patience is a superpower that shapes both our immediate reactions and our children's long-term character. Whether dealing with tantrums, sibling rivalries, or the stress of daily logistics, the capacity to remain calm can transform chaotic moments into teachable ones. By embodying patience in the mundane—waiting for a child to tie their shoelaces or allowing them space to make and learn from mistakes—parents create an environment of trust and emotional safety. Over time, patience becomes the silent force that nurtures cooperation, empathy, and enduring bonds within the family.

The Nature of Patience in Parenting
Patience as an Active Virtue

In the realm of parenting, patience emerges as an active virtue, a dynamic force rather than a passive state of being. This understanding elevates patience from a mere waiting game into a conscious practice, a deliberate choice that requires immense strength and resolve. It is a commitment to remaining composed in the face of frustration, a recognition that the turmoil of immediate emotional reactions can cloud judgment and lead to decisions that might undermine the very development one seeks to nurture in a child.

To embody patience is to acknowledge the complexities of parenting and the individuality of each child. It is an exercise in restraint, resisting the instinct to intervene at every turn, to "fix" the myriad challenges that arise in the developmental journey. Instead, a patient parent stands as a guide, providing a safe space for children to explore, stumble, and ultimately find their footing. This approach cultivates an environment in which children can learn and grow at their own pace, fostering not only their confidence but also their independence.

Stoic philosophy, with its emphasis on self-mastery and the control of one's impulses, resonates deeply within this framework of patience. The Stoics recognized that true strength lies not in the absence of emotion but in the ability to navigate those emotions without allowing them to dictate one's actions. In the context of parenting, this perspective invites parents to embrace moments of frustration as opportunities for growth—both for themselves and for their children. Each moment of restraint is a testament to the understanding that the process of growth is often non-linear, rich with lessons that can only be gleaned through experience.

Thus, patience becomes a profound act of love and wisdom. It transforms the parent-child relationship into a partnership of discovery, where the child is empowered to face challenges and learn from them. As parents exercise patience, they not only foster resilience in their children but also embody a powerful lesson in the virtue of waiting—waiting for the right moment, waiting for understanding to blossom, and waiting for growth to unfold naturally. In this light, patience is not merely a passive stance; it is a powerful engagement with the unfolding narrative of life, one that honors both the parent and the child as they navigate the intricate dance of development together.

The story of the Bamboo's slow growth

In some Eastern stories, there's a fascinating tale about bamboo. It gets planted and, for what feels like a long time, nothing seems to happen—no little shoots, no signs of growth. But underground, its roots are busy spreading out and getting stronger. Once it's ready, bamboo can shoot up to incredible heights, showing us the importance of that hidden work that happens first. Just like bamboo takes its time to build those roots, the results of parenting don't always show up right away. We're busy instilling values, setting routines, and providing emotional support, often left wondering if it's making a difference. It's important to embrace patience, understanding that slow, unseen growth is part of the journey. Each small lesson and every act of love we share helps shape our child's character, even if we can't see it yet. Eventually, that quiet foundation will emerge as confident and caring behavior. Keeping this in mind helps us stay positive and reminds us that our consistent efforts—like watering that bamboo—are nurturing something beautiful for the future. What might seem still today could be the start of something amazing tomorrow.

Why Impatience Arises

Impatience, that familiar companion of modern existence, often arises as a response to the cacophony of daily demands. In the realm of parenting, where responsibilities multiply like shadows at dusk, stress and urgency become the air one breathes. The relentless pursuit of harmony amidst chaos breeds an atmosphere where the virtues of patience are frequently overshadowed by the pressing need for immediate results.

The imposition of unrealistic expectations—such as the desire for instant compliance—serves to stoke the flames of frustration. This desire for immediacy reflects a deeper yearning for control in an unpredictable world. It is a manifestation of our own insecurities, projecting onto our children the belief that their actions must align perfectly with our expectations. Such a stance is not merely a reflection of the present moment but an echo of societal pressures that dictate success, often measured by swift outcomes rather than the gradual cultivation of understanding and growth.

Further complicating this landscape is the fear of judgment from others. In public spaces, the gaze of relatives and onlookers can amplify feelings of inadequacy, turning simple moments into battlegrounds of perception. The weight of societal scrutiny can transform a child's innocent exploration into a source of anxiety for the parent, leading to an impatience that is less about the child's behavior and more about protecting one's own self-image. In these moments, the pursuit of validation can overshadow the fundamental purpose of parenting: nurturing and guiding a young mind.

Moreover, the inherent mismatch between children's developmental stages and the adult world's rigid timelines often creates a chasm of misunderstanding. Adults, burdened by the clock and societal expectations, may forget that a child's learning unfolds at its own pace, governed by curiosity rather than the urgency of grown-up agendas. This discord invites impatience to thrive, as the adult mind struggles to reconcile the fluidity of childhood with the structured demands of life.

Recognizing these triggers is the first step toward transcending impatience. It invites a shift in perspective, urging us to embrace understanding over judgment. To acknowledge that each moment of impatience reveals not only our struggles as caregivers but also the profound complexity of human development. In this recognition lies the potential for growth, where the transformative power of empathy can flourish, allowing patience to become a guiding principle rather than a fleeting aspiration. Thus, the journey from impatience to understanding can be viewed not merely as a necessity but as a philosophical endeavor, one that enriches both parent and child in their shared experience of existence.

Setting Realistic Timelines

Setting realistic timelines is crucial for fostering a supportive environment where children can thrive in their daily routines and learning experiences. By incorporating extra minutes into morning routines, parents can significantly alleviate the stress that often leads to snapping or frustration. A calm, unhurried start to the day not only sets a positive tone but also encourages both parents and children to connect more peacefully. Children thrive when given ample time to process instructions, especially when they are introduced to new tasks. Rushing through these critical moments can impede understanding and retention. By embracing a slower pace, parents empower their children to absorb information fully and ask questions, resulting in a more enriching learning experience. It's essential to acknowledge that developmental milestones vary widely among children. While some may quickly master certain skills, others may require more time to do so. Recognizing these differences is key to adjusting schedules in a way that respects each child's unique learning journey. This approach nurtures self-esteem and reinforces the idea that growth is a personal journey, not a race. Adapting your timetable based on these insights showcases proactive patience. It helps avoid unnecessary frustrations for both parent and child, fostering a more harmonious household. By understanding and accommodating individual learning speeds, parents can create an environment that cultivates confidence, resilience, and a genuine love for learning.

The Ripple Effect of Patient Behavior

In the delicate tapestry of childhood development, the threads of behavior are often woven from the experiences children witness in their immediate environments. When faced with frustration, children become keen observers of their caregivers, absorbing not only actions but also the emotional responses that accompany them. The capacity to remain calm in the face of adversity is not merely a skill; it is a profound lesson in resilience and composure that shapes a child's ability to navigate life's inevitable challenges.

Patience, in its most genuine form, acts as a powerful antidote to the chaos that can arise from frustration. When caregivers respond to stressful situations with calmness, they set a precedent for their children, illustrating that emotional regulation is not just a necessity, but a choice. This choice becomes a beacon during times of tension, illuminating a path that de-escalates potential conflicts before they can take hold. It transforms what could be a power struggle into an opportunity for understanding and growth, teaching children that patience can diffuse anger and foster harmony.

The environment of a patient household cultivates a sanctuary of emotional safety. Children thrive when they feel secure, and consistent calm interactions provide a foundation for trust and open communication. In such an environment, feelings are validated, and vulnerabilities are met with kindness, allowing children to express themselves freely without fear of judgment. This emotional safety net nurtures the development of self-esteem and encourages children to approach the world with confidence and curiosity.

The impact of this patient behavior extends far beyond the four walls of the home. The lessons learned in a nurturing environment are carried into schools and social settings, where children engage with peers and authority figures. The ability to remain calm under pressure, to respond with empathy rather than reaction, becomes a tool that they wield throughout their lives. As they navigate friendships and academic challenges, the principles of patience and understanding guide their interactions, fostering relationships built on mutual respect.

Over time, the cultivation of patience within the household becomes a ripple that spreads outward, influencing not only the child but also the broader community. A patient home fosters an atmosphere where empathy flourishes, where the values of respect and open dialogue are prioritized. As children grow into adults, they carry these values with them, contributing to a society that values patience, understanding, and cooperative problem-solving.

In essence, the ripple effect of patient behavior is profound. It shapes not only the individual child but also the collective fabric of society, creating a legacy of compassion and resilience that can transcend generations. By choosing patience, caregivers not only enrich their own lives but also empower the next generation to embrace the beauty of calmness and respect in an often tumultuous world.

Long-Term Benefits of Practicing Patience

Practicing patience yields profound long-term benefits that can transform not just individual lives, but entire family dynamics. First and foremost, a tranquil family atmosphere significantly reduces stress levels, fostering a mental environment conducive to well-being for all family members. When parents model patience, children absorb this behavior, leading to a calmer home where anxiety is diminished.

Moreover, patience cultivates greater resilience in both children and parents. Life is full of challenges, and those who practice patience develop the ability to navigate difficulties with composure. This resilience is invaluable; it empowers families to face obstacles together, reinforcing a sense of unity and strength.

Additionally, patience enhances problem-solving capabilities. In high-stress situations, it's easy to become overwhelmed and reactive. However, when tensions are low, families can brainstorm solutions collaboratively, leading to more effective and creative outcomes. This collaborative spirit not only resolves issues but also strengthens the family's problem-solving skills as a unit.

The bonds formed through patience are also noteworthy. When children witness their struggles being met with support rather than anger, it fosters deep trust. This trust creates a safe space for open communication, allowing relationships to flourish. Over time, these strong bonds translate into a supportive network that can weather life's storms together.

Lastly, instilling patience in children is a gift that lasts a lifetime. Kids raised with patient guidance often grow into empathetic adults, capable of managing their emotions and understanding others. This lifelong skill not only benefits them personally but also enriches their interactions with the world around them.

In conclusion, the long-term benefits of practicing patience are undeniable. By cultivating a patient environment, families can reduce stress, build resilience, improve problem-solving, strengthen bonds, and equip children with essential life skills. Embracing patience is not just an immediate strategy; it is a powerful investment in the future of every family member.

Techniques to Strengthen Patience
Mindful Breathing and Pauses

In our fast-paced world, cultivating patience is not just a virtue but a necessity. One of the most effective methods to strengthen this trait is through mindful breathing and intentional pauses. Imagine a simple breathing exercise: you inhale slowly, hold for a few seconds, and then exhale. This practice can serve as a powerful reset when impatience begins to rise. By integrating a mental mantra, such as "I choose calm," you reinforce your ability to control emotions and reactions.

Encouraging children to adopt similar breathing techniques can set them on a path of self-regulation from an early age. When they observe adults practicing these techniques, they learn the invaluable skill of pausing before reacting. Over time, these quick interventions can become second nature, allowing individuals to navigate challenging situations with composure and clarity.

Such conscious pauses align beautifully with Stoic philosophy, which emphasizes the importance of reason over impulsive emotion. By cultivating a habit of mindful breathing, we can rise above frustration and irritation, making patience a cornerstone of our character. Ultimately, these techniques not only enhance our personal well-being but also foster a more harmonious environment for everyone around us.

Re-framing Frustrating Moments

In the journey of parenting and education, the moments that can incite frustration often reveal deeper opportunities for growth and understanding. When a child moves at a slow pace, it is tempting to interpret this behavior as defiance. However, if we consciously choose to reframe our perspective, we can see this as a natural part of their learning curve. Rather than asking, "Why won't you hurry?" we can shift our inquiry to, "They are discovering how to navigate this task; how can I support them?"

This simple but profound shift in mindset reduces the tendency to assign blame, allowing us to cultivate empathy instead. When we view the situation through a lens of support, we open ourselves to constructive guidance. We begin to recognize that each moment of perceived slowness is not a challenge to our authority or an interruption of our plans, but rather an opportunity for a child to engage deeply with their learning process.

Reframing these frustrating moments not only benefits the child but also lowers our own stress levels. By focusing on solutions rather than obstacles, we create a more harmonious environment conducive to growth. This perspective encourages a collaborative atmosphere, where both the adult and the child can thrive.

Psychologically, this technique fosters more positive and forward-thinking interactions. It encourages us to embrace patience and curiosity, allowing us to connect with children on a deeper level. When we approach learning as a shared journey rather than a race against time, we nurture an intrinsic motivation within the child. They learn that exploration and understanding are valued over mere speed, instilling a love for learning that will serve them far beyond any individual task.

Ultimately, reframing frustrating moments transforms the dynamic of our interactions, paving the way for a more empathetic and supportive relationship. By choosing to see the potential in these moments, we not only empower our children but also enrich our own experience as guides in their developmental journey.

Managing Expectations

Managing expectations is a fundamental aspect of fostering a healthy environment for children, one that acknowledges their unique developmental stages and individual temperaments. It is essential to critically assess whether the demands we place upon them regarding time, behavior, or skill level align with their age and inherent characteristics. When we impose expectations that exceed their capabilities, we risk creating a sense of inadequacy, which can stifle their natural curiosity and eagerness to learn.

The complexity of daily routines can lead to overwhelming situations for children. By simplifying these routines, we reduce the load on their young minds and hearts. A less hurried pace not only diminishes the potential for conflict but also creates a space where children can thrive. In this slower rhythm, we find room for patience, understanding, and connection—elements that are crucial for healthy development.

Clear communication of expectations is equally vital. Children must comprehend what is required of them if they are to navigate their responsibilities effectively. When we articulate our expectations with clarity, we provide them with a roadmap for success, enabling them to understand their roles and the parameters within which they can operate. This clarity fosters a sense of security and confidence, which is essential for their growth.

Moreover, recognizing and celebrating small wins or improvements cultivates a positive reinforcement cycle. It is imperative to instill in children the belief that effort is valued more than the pursuit of perfection. In a culture that often glorifies instant success, we must emphasize the importance of persistence and resilience. By acknowledging their progress, however minor, we encourage a mindset that appreciates the journey of growth rather than fixating solely on the destination.

The delicate balance between ambition and empathy is the cornerstone of nurturing an environment conducive to growth. While it is natural to aspire for our children to achieve great things, we must temper this ambition with a deep understanding of their emotional and psychological needs. When we create a space where they feel supported and understood, we empower them to reach for their potential without the fear of failure. In such an environment, growth becomes not just a possibility but an achievable reality, allowing children to flourish in their unique ways.

Using Timers and Visual Cues

Timers and visual cues represent a profound shift in how we can approach the concept of time management, particularly in the context of nurturing children's independence. By employing these tools, we can transcend the often fraught dynamics of parental reminders, which can feel nagging and intrusive. Instead, we create an environment where children can intuitively grasp the boundaries of time through visual and auditory signals, fostering a sense of agency and self-regulation.

These timers and charts serve as objective markers for tasks, transforming the anxiety often associated with deadlines into clear and manageable steps. When children see a countdown or a progress bar, they are not merely being told to hurry up; they are engaging with a system that visually represents their journey toward completion. This not only alleviates stress but also enhances their understanding of time as a resource to be managed rather than a looming pressure.

Moreover, the use of color-coded charts can be particularly impactful. Colors evoke emotions and can stimulate a child's motivation to complete tasks. By associating specific colors with various stages of a task, we provide not just direction but also encouragement. This multisensory approach taps into their innate curiosity and desire for accomplishment, making the process of task completion not just a necessity but a fulfilling experience.

The autonomy granted to children through these methods is invaluable. When they track their own progress, they are not merely passive recipients of instructions; they become active participants in their own learning. This fosters a sense of responsibility that is crucial for their development. They learn to manage their time and tasks, skills that are essential not only in childhood but throughout life.

Furthermore, the adoption of timers and visual cues liberates parents from the burden of constant verbal reminders. This shift is not just about efficiency; it preserves emotional energy and promotes a healthier family dynamic. Without the need to repeatedly remind or urge, parents can engage more meaningfully with their children, nurturing relationships built on trust and understanding rather than frustration and impatience.

By embracing these innovative tools, we invite a more harmonious interaction with time, one that empowers children while simultaneously relieving parents. In this philosophical pursuit of balance, we recognize that time, when visualized and understood, becomes a bridge to growth rather than a barrier to connection.

Practicing Shared Problem-Solving

Practicing shared problem-solving transcends the archaic model of authority and obedience, inviting a paradigm shift in how we engage with children. By adopting a collaborative approach—prompting children with questions like, "We need to leave in 10 minutes—what do you need to do first?"—we empower them to take ownership of their responsibilities. This engagement transforms them from passive recipients of directives into active participants in their own learning and decision-making processes.

Involvement is not merely a technique; it is a philosophy that nurtures a deeper sense of accountability and autonomy in children. When children feel that their input matters, they develop a genuine investment in the tasks at hand. This ownership fosters a sense of pride and accomplishment that is far more enduring than any fleeting satisfaction derived from compliance. In this shared endeavor, children become partners, learning to navigate challenges together, rather than succumbing to the rigidity of a command-and-obey mentality.

Moreover, this collaborative dynamic cultivates patience. By moving away from a simplistic binary of authority, we encourage a more nuanced understanding of how to plan and achieve goals together. In doing so, children not only learn how to manage their time effectively but also hone their critical thinking skills. They engage in discussions, weigh options, and explore possibilities, ultimately co-creating solutions that reflect their unique perspectives. This process of negotiation and cooperation is not just an academic exercise; it is a fundamental life skill that will serve them well beyond childhood.

The reduction of power struggles is perhaps one of the most profound benefits of this approach. When children feel respected as collaborators, the adversarial nature of traditional hierarchies diminishes. This fosters an atmosphere of mutual respect, where ideas can flow freely, and differences can be navigated constructively. As we embrace this philosophy, we equip children with the tools to communicate effectively, resolve conflicts, and build relationships based on trust and understanding.

In conclusion, practicing shared problem-solving is not merely an educational strategy; it is a transformative approach that shapes the very fabric of our interactions with children. It invites them to step into their roles as capable individuals, ready to face the complexities of life with confidence and insight. By fostering a culture of collaboration, we not only enhance their skills but also cultivate a future generation that values partnership, empathy, and shared responsibility.

Handling Conflict with Composure
The Stoic Approach to Conflict

The Stoic approach to conflict invites us to embrace the inevitability of discord as a fundamental aspect of human interaction. Conflict is not an enemy to be vanquished but rather a natural phenomenon that, when approached with the right mindset, can foster growth and understanding. In the realm of parenting, this perspective is particularly poignant. Children often find themselves caught in the crossfire of competing desires—bedtime versus playtime, homework versus leisure. These moments of contention are not mere obstacles; they are opportunities for teaching resilience, empathy, and the art of negotiation.

When we view conflict through a neutral lens, we strip away the emotional weight that often clouds our judgment. This reframing allows us to respond rather than react. By cultivating an environment where conflict is seen as a chance to learn—about ourselves, our children, and the dynamics of our relationships—we foster a culture of open dialogue and mutual respect. Such an approach diminishes the emotional charge that often escalates disputes, allowing for constructive conversations rather than heated arguments.

Maintaining composure in the face of conflict is a testament to dignity and self-control. These are virtues that children observe and internalize, shaping their own responses to adversity. A parent who remains calm amidst a storm of disagreement models the behavior they wish to instill. This calmness serves as a beacon, guiding children through the tumult of their own challenges, teaching them that it is not the conflict itself that defines us, but rather how we choose to navigate it.

This Stoic philosophy finds resonance in modern conflict-resolution strategies, which underscore the importance of calm and empathetic dialogue. Just as Stoics taught that our perceptions shape our reality, contemporary approaches to conflict emphasize the power of listening, understanding, and responding with compassion. By embodying these principles, we not only handle our own conflicts with grace but also equip our children with the tools they need to face their own challenges with wisdom and poise. In nurturing a mindset that embraces conflict as an opportunity for growth, we prepare our children for a world where understanding and cooperation are paramount.

De-Escalation Techniques

In the realm of parenting and conflict resolution, the adoption of de-escalation techniques emerges not just as a practical necessity but as a profound philosophical approach to nurturing emotional intelligence in children. Reflective listening stands as a cornerstone of this methodology. By restating your child's concerns, you engage in an act of empathy that transcends mere words. It fosters a connection rooted in understanding, signaling to the child that their feelings are worthy of recognition. This practice cultivates an environment where dialogue flourishes, rather than one where silence and resentment fester.

Lowering your voice is another essential technique that operates on a deeper psychological level. A softer tone can act as a balm to a heated situation, disarming aggression and inviting a more thoughtful exchange. It is a reminder that authority does not require volume; rather, true strength lies in the ability to remain calm amidst chaos. This shift in tone encourages children to mirror this behavior, instilling in them the value of measured responses, even when emotions run high.

Validating feelings is perhaps one of the most crucial aspects of effective communication. Acknowledging a child's frustration, regardless of the circumstances, affirms their emotional experience. This validation is not an endorsement of negative behavior but rather a compassionate acknowledgment of their humanity. It teaches children that emotions are complex and that feeling frustrated does not invalidate their worth or the necessity of rules. By creating space for this emotional validation, parents can guide their children towards healthier expressions of discontent.

Offering choices rather than imposing directives is a philosophical pivot towards empowerment. It transforms the dynamic from one of authority to collaboration. By presenting acceptable alternatives, parents not only respect their child's autonomy but also teach them critical decision-making skills. This approach fosters a sense of agency, allowing children to feel more in control of their circumstances while still aligning with the necessary boundaries set by their parents.

Each of these de-escalation techniques serves as a foundational pillar in teaching children to communicate effectively. They pivot conflicts away from confrontation and towards constructive dialogue, laying the groundwork for emotional resilience and interpersonal skills. In cultivating these attributes, we prepare our children not just to navigate familial disputes, but to engage with the world around them in a manner that values understanding, respect, and cooperation. Thus, these techniques are not merely strategies; they are philosophies that shape the very essence of human interaction.

Transforming Power Struggles into Teachability

Transforming power struggles into teachable moments requires a shift in perspective, recognizing that these conflicts are rooted in a child's intrinsic desire for autonomy. When a child asserts their independence, it often collides with parental control, creating an environment ripe for conflict. However, this clash is not merely a battle of wills but an opportunity for deeper understanding and connection.

At the heart of these struggles is the fundamental need for independence and the desire to be heard. Instead of engaging in surface-level arguments that perpetuate a cycle of resistance and authority, we must delve into the underlying emotions and motivations driving these behaviors. By acknowledging a child's need for autonomy, we can guide them toward expressing their needs in healthier, constructive ways. For instance, saying, "I see you want freedom; let's discuss safe ways to gain it," opens a dialogue that respects their feelings while establishing boundaries.

This approach not only mitigates conflict but also models essential problem-solving skills. Rather than asserting authority through sheer power, parents can cultivate an environment where respect and collaboration thrive. Children learn that their voices matter and that their desires can be negotiated within a safe framework. This respectful engagement fosters a sense of agency in children, allowing them to feel valued and understood even when their wishes are not fully met.

Moreover, when children experience their perspectives being considered, they develop a stronger sense of self-esteem. The knowledge that their thoughts and feelings are acknowledged, even if they do not always lead to the outcomes they desire, empowers them. It creates a foundation of trust between parent and child, reinforcing the idea that their autonomy can coexist with guidance and support.

In transforming power struggles into teachable moments, we cultivate not only mutual respect but also resilience in our children. They learn that negotiation and understanding are powerful tools for navigating relationships. These lessons extend beyond the parent-child dynamic, equipping them with the skills needed to engage with the world around them thoughtfully and em-pathetically. Ultimately, this shift in approach benefits everyone involved, fostering growth, understanding, and a deeper connection that transcends conflict.

Responding to Extreme Behaviors

In contemplating the response to extreme behaviors such as tantrums, shouting, or defiance, one finds oneself at the intersection of emotion and reason. The natural parental instinct may lean towards an immediate reaction—shouting back or meting out harsh punishment. Yet, this impulse raises profound questions about authority, empathy, and the nature of discipline.

To respond with a firm yet calm demeanor is to embrace a philosophy rooted in understanding rather than reaction. It acknowledges the child's emotional landscape, recognizing that their outburst is not merely a challenge to parental authority but a manifestation of their inner turmoil. By validating their feelings while simultaneously establishing boundaries, parents engage in a delicate dance of communication. This approach reflects a deeper truth: emotions need not be suppressed but understood and guided.

Removing a child from an overstimulating environment speaks to the importance of context in emotional regulation. It suggests that our surroundings significantly influence our behavior and that space can serve as a sanctuary for reflection and composure. This act of separation is not an abandonment of the child's feelings but rather a compassionate recognition of their need for tranquility.

Once the storm of emotions has subsided, the reflective dialogue that follows offers a vital opportunity for growth. Together, the parent and child can explore the roots of the outburst, fostering a shared understanding that transcends mere reprimand. This collaborative reflection invites the child into a process of self-discovery, where they learn to identify triggers and develop strategies for future encounters.

In consistently addressing extreme behaviors with patience, parents impart lessons of self-regulation and responsibility. This pedagogical approach cultivates a sense of agency within the child, empowering them to navigate their emotions with greater awareness. It posits that the journey of emotional growth is not solely the parent's responsibility but a shared exploration, where both parties learn the art of compassion, restraint, and understanding.

Ultimately, this philosophy of response embodies a vision of parenting that seeks not only to correct behavior but to nurture the emotional and moral development of the child. It posits that in the face of extreme behaviors, the path paved with patience and insight leads not only to individual growth but to a richer, more empathetic relationship between parent and child.

Long-Range Impact of Composed Conflict Resolution

The long-range impact of composed conflict resolution transcends immediate outcomes, weaving a profound tapestry of emotional intelligence that shapes the very essence of interpersonal relationships. Children who observe and engage in calm conflict resolution are not merely learning how to navigate disagreements; they are absorbing healthier communication patterns that will serve them throughout their lives. When these young minds witness their parents handle disputes with composure and respect, they internalize these behaviors, fostering a natural inclination toward understanding rather than aggression.

In a world where manipulation and stonewalling often masquerade as strength, these children emerge as beacons of empathy and reason. They learn that true power lies not in controlling others through intimidation or silence but in the ability to listen, understand, and articulate their feelings. This foundational skill set becomes a protective shield against the tumultuous storms of future relationships, allowing them to forge connections that are not only deeper but also more resilient.

The benefits ripple outward, affecting parents as well. As they practice composed conflict resolution, they experience a reduction in stress and a significant decrease in lingering resentments. The act of resolving conflicts constructively fosters an atmosphere of trust and safety, where family members feel heard and valued. This dynamic transforms conflicts from moments of tension into opportunities for growth and understanding, ultimately leading to stronger familial bonds.

Over time, what begins as a practice of conflict resolution evolves into a culture of open dialogue. Families that embrace this approach cultivate an environment where disagreements are not feared but welcomed as essential components of healthy relationships. By teaching that anger is not the key to control, this environment nurtures a collective understanding that reason and empathy are far more effective tools for resolution.

Thus, the long-range impact of composed conflict resolution extends beyond the immediate setting, embedding itself into the very fabric of society. As each generation learns to communicate with clarity and compassion, we move closer to a world where understanding prevails over conflict, and where human connections are cherished rather than fractured. It is imperative that we recognize the transformative power of this approach, not only for our families but for the broader community, paving the way for a future marked by harmonious interactions and lasting relationships.

Overcoming Challenges and Keeping Bonds Strong

Guiding Sibling Interactions

Sibling interactions can be a source of joy, learning, and connection when guided effectively. Sibling rivalries often arise from competition for attention, resources, or recognition, but these conflicts can be transformed into opportunities for growth. It is crucial to encourage siblings to voice their frustrations calmly and to actively listen to one another's perspectives. By fostering an environment where feelings can be expressed openly, children learn to navigate their emotions and understand each other better.

Using "I" statements can be a game changer in sibling communication. When a child says, "I feel upset when…" it shifts the focus from blame to personal feelings, opening a pathway for constructive dialogue rather than defensiveness. This technique not only reduces tension but also teaches valuable skills in expressing emotions and resolving conflicts.

Intervention is essential when conflicts escalate. Parents and caregivers should step in early to model constructive dialogue, preventing negativity from festering and escalating into deeper resentment. This proactive approach demonstrates to children that conflicts can be resolved amicably and that communication is key.

Reinforcing the values of patience and empathy is vital. When siblings learn to solve problems independently, they develop resilience and a deeper understanding of one another. By guiding these interactions and providing support, parents can help siblings cultivate a strong, positive relationship that will benefit them throughout their lives. Encouraging siblings to handle their disputes with care not only fosters a harmonious home environment but also equips them with essential life skills for future relationships.

Promoting Cooperative Activities

Promoting cooperative activities among siblings is essential for nurturing a harmonious family environment. Engaging in shared goals or projects, such as cooking a family meal or assembling a puzzle, not only fosters teamwork but also strengthens the bond between siblings. These activities provide a platform for children to learn the value of collaboration. When they work together towards a common goal, they experience the joy of collective achievement.

As siblings collaborate, they naturally practice patience. They learn to wait their turn, divide tasks, and understand that each person's contribution is vital to the success of the project. This process teaches them essential life skills that extend beyond the immediate activity, preparing them for future interactions in school and beyond.

It is crucial to recognize and praise moments of successful cooperation. Celebrating these achievements reinforces the notion that working together can be both enjoyable and rewarding. When children receive positive reinforcement, they are more likely to seek out cooperative experiences in the future, further solidifying their teamwork skills.

Inevitably, friction may arise during these activities. Instead of scolding, parents should guide siblings to brainstorm solutions together. This approach not only diffuses tension but also empowers the children to navigate conflicts constructively. By encouraging them to communicate and collaborate on resolving issues, parents help cultivate problem-solving skills and emotional intelligence.

Over time, positive cooperative experiences will overshadow petty rivalries and disagreements. As siblings learn to appreciate each other's strengths and contributions, they develop mutual respect. This foundation of respect is invaluable, shaping their relationships for years to come. By promoting cooperative activities, parents can create an environment where teamwork thrives, setting the stage for lifelong bonds and shared memories.

Encouraging Shared Problem-Solving

Encouraging shared problem-solving among siblings fosters a profound sense of agency and responsibility. When we pose the question, "How do each of you think we can fix this?" we invite them to step into the realm of negotiation, a space where their voices matter and their perspectives are valued. This not only cultivates their ability to articulate their feelings and desires but also instills a fundamental respect for the needs of others.

In this process, siblings are not just resolving conflicts; they are learning essential life skills that transcend their immediate disputes. Patience, compromise, and perspective-taking become second nature, echoing the Stoic virtues that guide us toward a more harmonious existence. The practice of patience teaches them that solutions often require time and contemplation, while compromise encourages the understanding that no solution is perfect, yet many can be satisfactory. Perspective-taking enriches their emotional intelligence, allowing them to see beyond their own immediate desires and consider the feelings and needs of their siblings.

Conflict, while often viewed as a negative experience, is, in fact, a normal aspect of human relationships. By framing conflicts as opportunities for growth and mutual understanding, we remind our children that resolution is not only possible but can be achieved amicably through effort and empathy. This shift in perspective transforms disputes from battlegrounds into collaborative endeavors, where each sibling is a partner in crafting a solution.

As siblings engage in this practice of shared problem-solving, the need for parental intervention diminishes. Children become more autonomous, embracing the responsibility that comes with resolving their own issues. This autonomy is essential for their development, as it empowers them to navigate the complexities of relationships with confidence and skill. They learn that while they may not always agree, they possess the tools to reach a consensus, fostering a sense of unity despite their differences.

By encouraging this approach, we are not merely addressing the immediate conflict; we are nurturing a generation that values cooperation, empathy, and thoughtful dialogue. In a world that often feels divided, the ability to negotiate solutions that honor the needs of all parties is a precious skill—one that can lead to lasting harmony not just within the family but in wider society as well.

When to Intervene vs. Step Back

Constant refereeing can significantly hinder children's development of essential self-regulation and conflict-resolution skills. It is crucial for children to learn how to navigate disagreements and resolve conflicts on their own. By stepping back during mild disagreements, parents and caregivers allow children to practice these skills in real-time. When children seem capable of handling the situation, stepping back empowers them to find their own solutions, fostering a sense of independence and confidence.

However, there are moments when intervention is necessary. If a conflict escalates and there is potential for harm, it is vital to step in calmly. Guiding children to cool down and discuss the situation helps them understand the importance of managing their emotions and addressing conflicts constructively. This approach not only protects them physically and emotionally but also reinforces the idea that seeking help is acceptable when needed.

Encouraging apologies and reconciliation processes after disagreements is equally important. Teaching children that relationships require mending after disputes instills valuable lessons about empathy, accountability, and the importance of maintaining healthy connections. By emphasizing the need to repair relationships, children learn that conflicts do not have to lead to lasting resentment but can instead be opportunities for growth and understanding.

Finding the right balance between intervening and stepping back is key to nurturing sibling relationships. This approach fosters independence while ensuring that children do not feel neglected or resentful. It is about guiding them towards becoming resilient individuals who can navigate their social environments effectively. Ultimately, promoting self-regulation and conflict resolution prepares children for future interpersonal relationships, equipping them with tools that will serve them throughout their lives.

Long-Term Benefits of Patient Sibling Dynamics

The long-term benefits of patient sibling dynamics cannot be overstated. Siblings who cultivate patience early in life are often primed to enter adulthood with stronger, more supportive relationships. This foundational skill fosters a sense of loyalty and understanding, allowing them to navigate the complexities of life as allies rather than adversaries.

When children observe their parents modeling composure in the face of challenges, they internalize these lessons. Such an environment significantly reduces the likelihood of perpetual rivalry, replacing competition with collaboration. Instead of constantly vying for attention or approval, siblings learn to appreciate each other's strengths and weaknesses, fostering a sense of unity. This shift from rivalry to support is crucial, as it lays the groundwork for enduring relationships.

Cooperative sibling interactions are fertile ground for the development of essential life skills such as teamwork, effective communication, and conflict resolution. These experiences provide a rich tapestry from which children can draw as they encounter diverse social situations. The ability to handle disagreements with grace is a skill that transcends family dynamics, enhancing their capabilities in friendships, academic partnerships, and future professional environments.

Furthermore, a patient and nurturing sibling relationship enhances each child's emotional intelligence. As they learn to empathize with one another's feelings and perspectives, they become adept at managing their own emotions. This emotional acuity translates into healthier peer relationships, where understanding and compassion replace misunderstandings and resentment. Siblings who have navigated the complexities of their interactions are often better equipped to forge meaningful connections outside the family unit.

Ultimately, siblings who develop patience and understanding towards one another evolve into allies and confidants. Their bond is anchored by mutual understanding, trust, and respect rather than competition. This profound connection serves as a sanctuary—an unwavering support system that enriches their lives long after childhood has passed. In a world often marked by individualism and strife, the patient dynamics cultivated between siblings offer a model of cooperation and solidarity that benefits not only the individuals involved but society as a whole. Investing in these relationships is not just about fostering harmony in the home; it is about nurturing future generations equipped to thrive together.

Sustaining a Patient Mindset Over Time
Periodic Self-Assessment

Sustaining a patient mindset over time is not just a lofty ideal; it's a necessary skill in our fast-paced world. Periodic self-assessment serves as the cornerstone of this endeavor. As we navigate our daily challenges, it becomes crucial to regularly gauge our stress levels. Patience is inherently more difficult to maintain when we are operating on empty. Recognizing the signs of depletion allows us to take proactive steps toward replenishing our reserves.

Consider the moments when your patience is most tested. Perhaps it's during a difficult conversation or when faced with unexpected delays. By identifying these triggers, you can brainstorm supportive strategies tailored to your needs. Simple techniques, like taking intentional breaks or engaging in breathing exercises, can significantly enhance your resilience. These practices not only help in regaining composure but also foster a deeper understanding of your emotional landscape.

Tracking your progress is equally vital. Celebrating small improvements, no matter how minor, reinforces your commitment to growth and sustains your motivation. Each step forward is a testament to your efforts, reinforcing the notion that patience is not a fixed trait but a skill that can be honed.

Additionally, it's essential to shift your perspective on setbacks. Instead of viewing them as failures, see them as opportunities for refinement. This mindset aligns perfectly with Stoic journaling practices, which emphasize reflection and continuous growth.

"The unexamined life is not worth living." This quote by Socrates invites profound reflection on the nature of existence, urging individuals to engage in self-inquiry and introspection. It emphasizes the importance of critical thinking and personal reflection in leading a meaningful life.

To delve deeper into this idea, one can consider the implications of living an unexamined life. Without reflection, individuals may fall into routine patterns, allowing societal norms and external influences to dictate their choices and values. This lack of introspection can lead to a sense of disconnection from one's true self, resulting in feelings of emptiness or dissatisfaction. The pursuit of superficial pleasures may temporarily mask these feelings, but ultimately, they do not fulfill the deeper human need for purpose and understanding.

Conversely, examining one's life encourages a deeper connection with personal beliefs, aspirations, and emotions. It fosters a greater awareness of one's impact on others and the world. Engaging in philosophical inquiry can illuminate pathways for growth and transformation, as individuals confront their fears, biases, and assumptions. This process is not always comfortable, as it often involves grappling with difficult truths and confronting aspects of oneself that may have been ignored or suppressed.

Moreover, the act of self-examination can lead to a more authentic existence. When individuals understand their motivations and values, they can make choices that align with their true selves rather than conforming to external expectations. This authenticity fosters genuine connections with others, as individuals are more likely to engage in meaningful relationships based on mutual understanding and respect.

In the context of societal issues, an examined life can also contribute to collective awareness and responsibility. As individuals reflect on their roles within larger systems—be it cultural, political, or economic—they become better equipped to advocate for justice and change. The philosophical pursuit of understanding can inspire action that transcends personal interests, promoting a more compassionate and equitable society.

Ultimately, Socrates' assertion serves as a reminder that the journey of self-discovery is essential to living a fulfilling life. The willingness to engage in philosophical contemplation not only enriches individual lives but also enhances the fabric of society as a whole, fostering a culture of reflection, empathy, and growth.

In conclusion, sustaining a patient mindset is an ongoing journey that requires self-awareness, strategic planning, and a compassionate perspective on your own growth. By committing to periodic self-assessment, you not only enhance your patience but also enrich your overall well-being.

Practicing Forgiveness and Humility

Practicing forgiveness and humility is essential in the journey of parenthood, a path fraught with challenges and imperfections. No parent can embody perfect patience at all times; it is an unrealistic expectation that leads only to frustration and disillusionment. When moments of impatience occur, the act of apologizing to a child is not merely an admission of fault; it is a profound lesson in mutual respect. This simple gesture teaches children that humility is not a weakness but a strength, a vital component of human relationships.

Acknowledging our shortcomings allows us to model vulnerability, illustrating that self-improvement is a continuous endeavor. It is crucial to forgive ourselves for these lapses in patience. Self-forgiveness opens the door to reflection, prompting us to consider how we might respond more thoughtfully in the future. This reflection is not an act of self-indulgence but a commitment to growth; it reinforces the notion that each day offers a new opportunity to learn and evolve.

When parents embrace this philosophy, they cultivate an environment where children feel safe to make mistakes. They learn to approach their own errors with compassion, understanding that imperfection is part of the human experience. This fosters resilience and encourages a mindset of resolve, empowering children to face their own challenges with grace. In this way, the practice of forgiveness and humility becomes a cornerstone of character development, shaping not only how children see themselves but also how they relate to others.

In essence, the journey of parenting is intertwined with the lessons of forgiveness and humility. It is a shared experience that nurtures growth, instilling values that children will carry into their own lives. By embodying these principles, parents do not merely teach; they inspire a legacy of compassion and understanding that transcends generations.

Seeking Support Networks

Engaging with parenting groups, online forums, or friends who face similar challenges is not just beneficial; it is essential. The reality is that parenting can be a rollercoaster of emotions, and sharing stories and strategies with others normalizes the ups and downs of maintaining patience. When you hear others articulate their struggles, it reassures you that you are not alone in your feelings. This connection fosters a sense of belonging and reminds you that every parent experiences moments of frustration and doubt.

A supportive community can provide fresh perspectives that can be transformative. Sometimes, simply hearing how someone else approached a similar situation can spark a new idea or strategy for you. These insights can lighten your emotional burdens, making it easier to navigate the challenges of parenting. Moreover, the relationships you build within these networks can serve as a safety net during tough times, offering encouragement and understanding when you need it most.

If feelings of anxiety or impatience become overwhelming, it is crucial to consider seeking professional help. A therapist or counselor can provide tools and strategies tailored to your situation, allowing you to manage emotions more effectively. Remember, stoicism does not imply that you should face struggles in isolation. Building connections with others not only strengthens your resilience but also enriches your parenting experience. Embracing a support network is a proactive step towards cultivating patience and emotional well-being, making the journey of parenting more enjoyable and fulfilling.

Revisiting Stoic Inspirations

In the pursuit of a tranquil existence, the wisdom of Stoicism serves as a beacon, illuminating the path of composure amid life's inevitable tumult. The beauty of Stoic thought lies in its simplicity and accessibility; a handful of well-chosen quotes or passages can evoke profound reflections, grounding us in moments of upheaval. Consider the Stoic reminder that while we cannot control external events, we can govern our responses to them. This principle, encapsulated in the teachings of Seneca and Marcus Aurelius, urges us to cultivate an inner fortress impervious to the chaos that surrounds us.

Engaging with the letters of Seneca and the contemplations of Aurelius not only offers renewed motivation but also establishes a dialogue with the past. These writings, steeped in the rich soil of philosophical inquiry, challenge us to reflect on our own lives. They beckon us to examine the nature of our desires and fears, encouraging a reevaluation of what truly matters. In moments of despair or confusion, returning to these texts can serve as a reminder that we are part of a continuum of seekers grappling with similar existential questions.

Incorporating Stoic reflections into our daily routines, whether at dawn or dusk, creates a sanctuary of thought that nurtures resilience. Morning reflections can set the tone for the day, reinforcing the notion that each challenge is an opportunity to practice virtue. Bedtime contemplation allows for the introspection necessary to process the day's events, fostering a sense of closure and acceptance. This rhythmic engagement with Stoic principles acts as a form of meditation, anchoring us in the present while fortifying our resolve to face whatever lies ahead.

These textual anchors, when revisited regularly, not only preserve momentum during challenging periods but also cultivate a mindset attuned to serenity. The wisdom imparted by Stoicism acts as a shield against the tempests of life, reminding us of our agency and the power of perception. Through consistent exposure to these enduring lessons, we fortify our mental resilience, ensuring that our composure becomes a habitual response rather than a sporadic achievement. In a world rife with uncertainty, the Stoic path invites us to find strength in our convictions and tranquility in our hearts, allowing us to navigate life's vicissitudes with grace.

Transforming Patience into a Family Value

Patience is not just a virtue; it is a collective family value that can shape our interactions and strengthen our bonds. By openly discussing patience with children, we invite them to weigh in on its significance, empowering them to understand its role in our lives. When children articulate their thoughts on patience, they begin to recognize its impact on their relationships and decision-making.

Stories of patient behavior abound in history, literature, and real life, serving as powerful examples for our family. Consider the tale of a historical figure like Nelson Mandela, who demonstrated immense patience during his years of imprisonment, holding onto hope and integrity. In literature, characters like Atticus Finch in "To Kill a Mockingbird" exemplify patience as they navigate difficult moral landscapes with grace. Sharing these stories not only inspires but also provides relatable contexts in which children can see patience in action.

To further instill this value, we can develop simple family mottos or affirmations that emphasize calmness. Phrases such as "We choose understanding over anger" can serve as daily reminders of our commitment to patience. These mottos create a framework for our family discussions and interactions, guiding us through conflicts and challenges with a focus on understanding and empathy.

Reinforcing instances of patient behavior we witness—whether it's waiting for a sibling to finish a task or handling frustration with grace—celebrates this quality and instills a sense of pride in our family. When we acknowledge and praise patience, we create an environment where it is valued, encouraging everyone to model this behavior.

As we consistently practice and discuss patience, it gradually becomes woven into our family identity. It guides our actions naturally, allowing us to respond to life's challenges with a calm and understanding approach. By making patience a shared value, we not only strengthen our family ties but also equip ourselves and our children with a vital skill that will serve them well throughout their lives. Embracing patience together transforms it into a cornerstone of our family ethos, fostering a nurturing and supportive environment for everyone.

Key Takeaways (Chapter Cheat Sheet)

1. Patience is an Active Strength

    - Far from passive waiting, it's a choice to remain calm and constructive in the face of challenges.

2. Techniques for Building Patience

    - Mindful pauses, reframing frustrations, and realistic expectations all prevent hasty reactions.

3. Composure in Conflict Shapes Resilience

    - Calm, empathetic conflict resolution teaches children the power of thoughtful communication.

4. Fostering Patient Sibling Interactions

- Guided cooperation and shared problem-solving equip children with lifelong social skills.
5. Sustaining a Patient Mindset

    - Regular self-checks, community support, and Stoic inspirations help preserve and deepen your commitment to patience.

Reflection Prompts

1. Journaling Exercise

    - Recall a recent scenario where you felt your patience slipping. What factors contributed (e.g., time pressure, fear of judgment)? How could you better address those factors in the future?
2. Family Discussion

    - Ask each family member to describe a moment they appreciated someone else's patience. How did it make them feel? What might have happened if impatience took over instead?
3. Action Step

    - Choose one "hot spot" in your daily routine—morning rush, bedtime, homework hour—and commit to practicing a specific patience-building technique (e.g., mindful breathing, reframing) for a week. Track the outcomes.

Patience is the quiet force that turns chaos into opportunity, unlocking empathy and sustainable growth within your family. By deliberately cultivating calm interactions—whether in daily tasks or sibling disputes—you lay the groundwork for a harmonious household where everyone feels understood and valued.

Five

Raising Emotionally Resilient Children

"It's not what happens to you, but how you react to it that matters."
— *Epictetus*

Epictetus, a Greek Stoic philosopher born into slavery, rose to become one of history's most revered moral teachers. This quote succinctly captures the essence of Stoicism: life is fraught with challenges, yet our internal response shapes our ultimate experience. Emotional resilience, then, isn't about avoiding hardship; it's about cultivating the mindset to face adversity without succumbing to defeat or despair.

From a broader philosophical and psychological lens, emotional resilience refers to one's ability to adapt well to stress, setbacks, and even trauma. In modern psychology, resilience is often linked to practices like reframing negative events, seeking social support, and maintaining a growth mindset. These align seamlessly with Stoic principles: viewing obstacles as opportunities for character development, recognizing what lies within our control, and refusing to let external circumstances dictate our inner peace.

For parents, nurturing emotional resilience in children is both a vital goal and an ongoing process. Children inevitably encounter disappointments—lost competitions, academic hurdles, friendship conflicts. By guiding them to view setbacks as learning experiences, you help them develop both courage and self-efficacy. A Stoic-based approach ensures that rather than shielding kids from every bump in the road, you empower them to navigate life's uncertainties with confidence and steady resolve.

Understanding Emotional Resilience

Defining Resilience

Raising emotionally resilient children necessitates a profound understanding of what emotional resilience truly entails. At its core, emotional resilience is not merely the ability to bounce back from adversity; it is a dynamic process that encompasses the capacity to confront stress with a constructive mindset. Rather than shying away from challenges or responding with anger, emotionally resilient individuals learn to navigate their feelings, channeling them into personal growth and adaptive strategies.

Defining resilience involves recognizing that it is a multifaceted construct. It encompasses the ability to endure hardships while maintaining a sense of hope and purpose. In children, this means cultivating an awareness that setbacks are not the end of the road but rather opportunities for learning and development. Each disappointment becomes a stepping stone, teaching them that they can emerge stronger and wiser. As the philosopher Friedrich Nietzsche famously stated, "That which does not kill us makes us stronger." This notion serves as a powerful reminder that resilience is forged through experience, not in the absence of struggle.

The journey towards emotional resilience begins with the recognition that feelings, whether joyful or painful, are integral to the human experience. Children must be taught that emotions do not signify weakness; instead, they are valuable signals that can inform decision-making and drive personal growth. By modeling healthy emotional expression, parents and caregivers can guide children in understanding that it is acceptable to feel sad, angry, or frustrated. The key lies in how these emotions are processed and acted upon.

As children learn to confront and articulate their feelings, they develop a toolkit of coping strategies that will serve them throughout their lives. This includes problem-solving skills, self-regulation techniques, and the ability to seek support when needed. The cultivation of these skills fosters a sense of agency, empowering children to navigate future challenges with confidence. When they encounter adversity, they are less likely to view themselves as victims and more likely to see themselves as active participants in their own lives.

Over time, the development of resilience becomes woven into the fabric of a child's identity. It is not simply a skill to be acquired; it evolves into a fundamental aspect of who they are. This transformation shapes their worldview, influencing how they approach obstacles and setbacks. A resilient child grows to understand that life is inherently unpredictable, filled with both triumphs and tribulations. This understanding fosters a growth mindset, where challenges are met with curiosity rather than dread, and where failures are reframed as lessons rather than conclusions.

In nurturing emotional resilience, we prepare children not just to survive life's storms but to dance in the rain. Through this philosophical lens, we recognize that resilience is not a destination but a lifelong journey, one that is enriched by the experiences we encounter along the way. In the words of Maya Angelou, "You may encounter many defeats, but you must not be defeated." This perspective encourages us to embrace the full spectrum of human emotion, guiding the next generation to not only withstand the trials of life but to thrive in the face of them.

Key Traits of Resilient Children

Optimism is a cornerstone trait of resilient children, shaping their perspectives and responses to life's challenges. These children view setbacks not as insurmountable obstacles, but as temporary hurdles that can be overcome. This belief system fosters a sense of hope and encourages them to persist in the face of adversity. When children hold an optimistic outlook, they are more likely to engage in problem-solving behaviors rather than succumbing to feelings of defeat. This positivity not only enhances their coping mechanisms but also influences those around them, creating a supportive environment that reinforces their resilience.

Adaptability is another crucial trait that enables children to thrive amidst change. Resilient children possess the ability to adjust their thoughts and behaviors in response to new circumstances without losing their core identity. This flexibility empowers them to embrace challenges and navigate transitions, from moving to a new school to adapting to a family change. By fostering adaptability, we equip children with the tools to approach life's uncertainties with confidence and grace. They learn that change is not something to fear, but rather an opportunity for growth and self-discovery.

Self-efficacy plays a pivotal role in developing resilience. Children who trust in their abilities to handle life's uncertainties are more likely to take on challenges and pursue their goals with determination. This belief in themselves fosters a proactive mindset, encouraging them to take initiative and seek solutions rather than retreating into inaction. By nurturing self-efficacy in children, we empower them to face difficulties head-on, reinforcing the notion that they are capable of overcoming obstacles and achieving success, no matter how daunting the situation may seem.

Emotional regulation is essential for resilient children, as it allows them to navigate their feelings without being overwhelmed by them. These children are adept at recognizing their emotions and understanding their impact on behavior. Rather than letting anger, sadness, or frustration dictate their actions, they employ strategies to manage these feelings constructively. This skill not only helps them maintain composure in challenging situations but also fosters healthier relationships with peers and adults. By teaching emotional regulation, we provide children with a vital tool that promotes resilience, enabling them to respond thoughtfully rather than react impulsively.

Finally, the ability to seek support is a hallmark of resilient children. They understand the importance of reaching out to trusted adults or peers for help when needed. This trait reflects an awareness that vulnerability is not a weakness but a crucial aspect of resilience. By learning how to effectively ask for assistance, children build strong support networks that can bolster their emotional well-being. Encouraging support-seeking behaviors reinforces the idea that they are not alone in their struggles and that collaboration can lead to solutions and healing.

In summary, the key traits of resilience—optimism, adaptability, self-efficacy, emotional regulation, and support-seeking—are integral to fostering a generation of children who can navigate life's challenges with confidence and strength. By cultivating these traits in children, we lay the groundwork for a future where they are equipped to face adversity, embrace change, and thrive in an ever-evolving world. Investing in the development of these characteristics is not just beneficial for the individual child; it creates a ripple effect that enhances communities, fostering environments where resilience is the norm rather than the exception.

The Stoic Link to Resilience

Stoicism, as a philosophical discipline, teaches us the art of resilience by guiding individuals to discern between what lies within their control and what does not. This dichotomy is central to cultivating an attitude of acceptance towards life's inherent uncertainties and challenges. The Stoics understood that while we cannot dictate external events, we retain the power over our responses and judgments.

"Life is 10% what happens to us and 90% how we react to it" Charles R. Swindoll. Reminds us that adopting a proactive and constructive mindset can empower us as parents to navigate challenges more effectively, transforming potential setbacks into opportunities for learning and development.

When imparting these principles to children, the Stoic emphasis on acceptance becomes a valuable tool for navigating life's adversities. By framing challenges as normal occurrences, parents can help children develop a robust mental framework. The practice of negative visualization, a technique employed by ancient Stoics, serves as a poignant example. By briefly contemplating worst-case scenarios, individuals can emotionally prepare themselves for potential difficulties, thus mitigating the shock when faced with reality. This practice, when adapted for children, may involve simple discussions about "Plan B"—a constructive way to explore alternative outcomes without instilling fear.

In this context, normalizing adversity teaches children that setbacks are not only inevitable but also integral to the human experience. This philosophy fosters a sense of confidence, as children learn that they possess the inner resources to adapt and respond to challenges. Rather than viewing obstacles as barriers, they begin to see them as stepping stones on the path to resilience. Through this lens, the Stoic approach becomes a foundational element in nurturing a mindset that embraces life's unpredictability with courage and grace. The resilient individual, shaped by these teachings, emerges not only better equipped to handle adversities but also enriched by the lessons that such experiences impart.

Why Resilience Matters in Childhood

Resilience matters in childhood because it is the bedrock upon which future success and well-being are built. Early experiences with adversity are not merely obstacles; they are invaluable lessons that teach children essential coping skills. These skills are not just useful for navigating childhood challenges; they become lifelong tools that equip individuals to face the complexities of adult life with confidence and adaptability.

Fostering resilience in children acts as a protective barrier against mental health struggles such as anxiety and depression. When children learn to bounce back from setbacks, they develop a robust mindset that shields them from the overwhelming weight of negative emotions. This mental fortitude is crucial, as it significantly reduces the likelihood of these debilitating conditions taking root in their lives.

Moreover, resilient children are more inclined to embrace challenges with enthusiasm. Whether trying out a new hobby or engaging in social opportunities, they approach these experiences with an open heart and mind. This willingness to step outside their comfort zones is not only enriching but also essential for personal growth. They cultivate a sense of adventure and curiosity that can lead to greater creativity and innovation in their pursuits.

The belief in their ability to handle challenges—expressed as "I can handle this"—serves to mitigate the excessive fear of failure that can paralyze many individuals. This mindset encourages children to take risks, learn from mistakes, and ultimately thrive. By understanding that failure is not a definitive endpoint but rather a stepping stone to success, they develop a healthy relationship with challenges that will serve them well throughout their lives.

Furthermore, resilience lays the groundwork for healthier adult relationships and career success. A resilient individual is more likely to communicate effectively, resolve conflicts amicably, and maintain a positive outlook in interpersonal interactions. These skills are invaluable in both personal and professional contexts, fostering environments of collaboration and support. Additionally, the ability to persevere in the face of obstacles often translates into greater achievements in one's career, as resilient individuals are not easily deterred by setbacks.

In summary, building resilience in childhood is not just beneficial; it is essential. It equips children with the necessary tools to navigate life's challenges, protects against mental health struggles, and cultivates a mindset that encourages growth and exploration. The long-term benefits are profound, influencing everything from personal relationships to career trajectories and overall well-being. Investing in the resilience of our children is an investment in a brighter, healthier future for all.

Common Misconceptions

Resilience is often misunderstood, leading to harmful myths that can hinder personal growth and emotional well-being. One prevalent misconception is that resilience means toughing it out alone. In reality, seeking help during challenging times is not a sign of weakness; rather, it is a courageous acknowledgment of our shared human experience. The act of reaching out demonstrates strength and fosters connections that can bolster one's capacity to navigate difficulties.

Another common myth is that resilient children never feel upset. This is far from the truth. Resilient individuals experience a full range of emotions; they simply do not allow themselves to remain trapped in those feelings. It is essential to recognize that feeling upset is a natural response to adversity. The key lies in how children learn to process and move through their emotions, equipping them with the tools to bounce back.

Furthermore, there is a belief that resilience is an innate trait, a quality that some are born with while others are not. This myth undermines the reality that resilience is a skill that can be developed over time with proper guidance and practice. Just as we cultivate physical strength through exercise, we can also build emotional resilience through learning, experience, and support.

Another misconception is that minimizing a child's feelings teaches them resilience. On the contrary, dismissing or belittling a child's emotions can be detrimental. Validating their feelings is crucial for healthy coping. When children know their emotions are heard and understood, they are more likely to develop the confidence and skills necessary to face life's challenges.

Lastly, the notion that shielding children from all adversity builds confidence is misleading. Overprotection can stunt children's coping skills, preventing them from developing the resilience they need to handle life's inevitable setbacks. Exposure to manageable challenges helps children learn how to navigate difficulties, fostering a sense of accomplishment and self-efficacy.

Understanding these myths and embracing the truths about resilience can empower both children and adults to cultivate a healthier, more adaptable approach to life's challenges. Resilience is not about enduring struggles in isolation but rather about recognizing and embracing the support of others, processing emotions, and learning to navigate adversity with confidence and skill.

Cultivating a Growth Mindset
Growth vs. Fixed Mindset

The concept of a growth mindset, as articulated by psychologist Carol Dweck, is pivotal in shaping how we view our abilities and potential. Those who embrace a growth mindset perceive their skills and intelligence not as fixed attributes but as qualities that can be developed over time. This perspective is not merely a motivational tool; it is a profound philosophical stance that aligns closely with the teachings of Stoicism, which emphasizes the importance of virtue, resilience, and personal growth.

Encouraging children to prioritize effort and learning over the notion of inherent talent is essential for developing resilience. When children understand that persistence and dedication are more critical than innate ability, they become equipped to face challenges head-on. This focus on effort fosters an environment where mistakes are not seen as failures but as opportunities for learning and growth. In this light, the journey of self-improvement becomes a noble pursuit, reinforcing the idea that our capabilities can expand through hard work and determination.

Stoic philosophy further enriches this dialogue by positing that virtues and capabilities are cultivated through practice. The Stoics teach us that character is forged in the crucible of adversity. Each challenge we face is not a threat to our self-worth but a chance to demonstrate and enhance our virtues. When we encounter obstacles, we are presented with the opportunity to rise above and become more resilient individuals. This shift in perspective allows us to redefine our relationship with failure; it is no longer an endpoint but a stepping stone on the path to personal development.

By fostering a growth mindset, we empower ourselves and future generations to view challenges as essential components of life's journey. This philosophical approach not only enhances our ability to cope with setbacks but also cultivates a deeper sense of purpose and fulfillment. Ultimately, embracing a growth mindset invites us to participate actively in our own evolution, transforming the way we engage with the world and with ourselves.

Praise the Process, Not Just the Result

Praise the process, not just the result. When we compliment children for their diligence, creativity, or perseverance, we plant seeds of intrinsic motivation that flourish over time. Instead of merely proclaiming, "You're so smart!" which can inadvertently create a fixed mindset, recognizing effort and strategy empowers children to take ownership of their learning journey. This approach emphasizes that success is not solely a product of innate intelligence but rather a culmination of hard work and thoughtful engagement.

When children hear praise that highlights their improvements, they are more likely to embrace challenges and view setbacks as opportunities for growth. This shift in focus fosters a love for learning that transcends the fear of failure. By valuing progress over immediate perfection, children cultivate resilience and adaptability—skills that will serve them throughout their lives.

In the spirit of Stoic philosophy, we understand that the journey is often more significant than the destination itself. Celebrating the practice of virtue—the consistent effort to improve, learn, and grow—teaches children to truly appreciate the process of development and self-discovery. This perspective nurtures in them the ability to find genuine joy in the act of learning, rather than solely in external accolades or grades. It instills a resilient mindset where the pursuit of knowledge and skill evolves into a lifelong endeavor, marked by an insatiable curiosity and a courageous willingness to embrace challenges, setbacks, and new experiences along the way.

By shifting our praise from static labels to dynamic qualities, we create an environment where children feel valued for their efforts. They learn that their actions, strategies, and persistence are what truly define their capabilities. This approach not only nurtures a healthier self-image but also equips them with the tools to navigate the complexities of life, ensuring they appreciate every step of their journey and recognize that true growth lies in the process.

Encouraging Curiosity and Experimentation

Encouraging curiosity and experimentation in children is not just beneficial; it is essential for their growth and development. By providing opportunities for kids to engage in new activities, we ignite their sense of adventure and exploration. When we allow them to try different pursuits—be it a new sport, a creative project, or an exciting science experiment—we empower them to embrace the unknown. These experiences are invaluable, teaching them about the world around them while honing their problem-solving skills. It is vital that these activities occur within safe boundaries, enabling children to take small risks without facing dire consequences. This balance ensures they feel secure while being inspired to step outside their comfort zones. We must emphasize that mistakes are not just acceptable; they are a normal part of the learning journey. By fostering an environment where children feel safe to experiment without fear of failure, we cultivate resilience and perseverance—qualities that are essential for navigating life's challenges.

When adults openly acknowledge that stumbling is part of learning, children begin to view their errors not as setbacks but as golden opportunities for growth. This shift in perspective is crucial, as it encourages a growth mindset, focusing on progress rather than mere performance. Modeling curiosity is another powerful way to nurture an inquisitive mindset in children. When adults share their own learning experiences and experiments, they send a clear message: curiosity knows no age limit. Discussing new interests, hobbies, or knowledge creates a culture of exploration at home. Children are natural imitators; when they see their caregivers engaging with the world, they are inspired to do the same.

This modeling can manifest in numerous ways—visiting museums, exploring nature, or engaging in lively discussions about new ideas and concepts. By creating a curious and open-minded household, we normalize the learning curve that accompanies new challenges. When curiosity is celebrated, it encourages children to ask questions and seek answers. This environment transforms obstacles into invitations to expand their skill set rather than viewing them as insurmountable barriers. By framing challenges in this manner, children come to understand that every experience, whether positive or negative, enriches their development and deepens their understanding of the world.

Ultimately, cultivating an atmosphere that treasures curiosity and experimentation equips children to approach life with enthusiasm and confidence. They become more adaptable, eager to embrace change, and willing to learn from their experiences. This solid foundation not only enhances their individual growth but also arms them with the skills necessary for lifelong learning and adaptability in an ever-evolving world.

Re-framing Failures as Feedback

Reframing failures as feedback is a powerful strategy that can transform how children perceive challenges and setbacks. Instead of viewing a poor test score or a lost game as a definitive mark of failure, we can guide them to uncover valuable lessons embedded within these experiences. This shift in perspective not only fosters a growth mindset but also empowers children to embrace learning opportunities.

Encouraging reflective questioning is key to this process. When we ask, "What worked?" and "What can we try differently next time?" we invite children to analyze their experiences critically. This inquiry helps them identify their strengths and areas for improvement, reinforcing the idea that every experience can teach us something. By focusing on the learning aspect rather than the outcome, we cultivate a sense of curiosity and resilience.

This approach aligns seamlessly with the principles of Stoicism, which teaches us to view adversity as a chance to refine our virtues and wisdom. Stoics believed that challenges are not merely obstacles; they are opportunities for growth. By instilling this philosophy in children, we enable them to see setbacks as stepping stones rather than stumbling blocks. Each small failure becomes a valuable lesson, sharpening their ability to navigate future challenges with greater confidence.

Repeated exposure to minor setbacks, paired with thoughtful guidance, serves to inoculate children against the fear of trying. As they learn to view failures as part of the journey, they become more willing to take risks and explore new avenues. Over time, this practice builds resilience, allowing them to adapt and thrive in the face of adversity.

Ultimately, by reframing failures as feedback, we equip children with the skills to approach life's challenges with a problem-solving mindset. They learn that resilience is not about avoiding failure but about embracing it, understanding that every setback is an opportunity to grow and evolve. This perspective not only prepares them for academic and athletic pursuits but also lays a foundation for lifelong adaptability and strength.

Setting, Incremental Goals

Setting realistic, incremental goals is essential for nurturing a child's confidence and fostering a positive mindset. When children are pressured with overly ambitious targets, they can quickly become discouraged and disengaged. Instead of overwhelming them with lofty expectations, it's crucial to break larger tasks into smaller, manageable steps. This approach not only makes the process less daunting but also allows children to experience a sense of mastery as they achieve each stage.

Celebrating each incremental success is vital in reinforcing the idea that progress, no matter how small, matters. By acknowledging these achievements, we instill a growth mindset in children, helping them understand that consistent effort leads to improvement. Each step forward builds their confidence and motivates them to continue striving for their goals.

Moreover, involving children in the goal-setting process fosters a sense of ownership and responsibility. When they participate in deciding their objectives, they are more likely to feel invested in the outcomes. This collaboration encourages them to take pride in their efforts and understand that big achievements are often the result of steady, persistent work rather than sudden leaps.

As children learn to appreciate the journey of incremental progress, they internalize the valuable lesson that success is not merely about reaching the finish line but about the steps taken along the way. This understanding equips them with the resilience and determination needed to tackle future challenges, preparing them for a lifetime of growth and achievement.

Teaching Emotional Coping Skills
Identifying and Naming Emotions

Teaching emotional coping skills is essential for children's development, and one of the most effective strategies is encouraging them to identify and name their emotions. By teaching children to label feelings such as frustration, sadness, excitement, and nervousness, we empower them to express their internal states rather than simply acting them out. This practice aligns with the Stoic philosophy, which emphasizes that awareness of emotions is the first step toward managing them effectively.

Using simple language or emotion charts can significantly aid younger children in this process. These tools help bridge the gap between emotions and words, allowing children to connect their feelings with appropriate labels. When a child can articulate "I feel frustrated" instead of throwing a tantrum, they are taking a crucial step toward emotional regulation.

Moreover, validating a child's feelings by saying something like, "I see that you're upset," not only fosters a sense of understanding and acceptance but also strengthens the emotional bond between the child and the caregiver. This kind of recognition is crucial as it helps children feel genuinely seen and heard, rather than being dismissed or misunderstood, which can often lead to feelings of isolation. Such validation is vital because it builds a strong foundation of trust and opens the door for more in-depth dialogue about emotions, encouraging children to express themselves openly and learn to regulate their feelings in a healthy manner.

Over time, regularly labeling emotions normalizes self-reflection in children. This practice not only helps them understand their feelings better but also reduces impulsive outbursts. As children learn to recognize and name their emotions, they develop a toolkit for coping with life's challenges, promoting resilience and emotional intelligence. By prioritizing the teaching of emotional coping skills, we equip the next generation with the necessary tools to navigate their feelings and foster healthier relationships with themselves and others.

Breathing and Visualization Techniques

Breathing and visualization techniques are essential tools for managing intense emotions and fostering resilience in children. One effective method is box breathing. This simple yet powerful exercise involves inhaling for a count of four, holding the breath for four, exhaling for four, and pausing for another four. Teaching kids this technique can provide them with immediate relief during moments of anxiety or stress. When they can calm their racing thoughts and emotions, they are better equipped to handle challenges.

Visualization is another impactful strategy. Encouraging children to imagine a peaceful place or envision a successful outcome can redirect anxious thoughts and foster a sense of control. This practice not only alleviates immediate worries but also enhances their ability to approach future challenges with confidence. By guiding them through these exercises, you are not just teaching them techniques; you are equipping them with a mental toolkit that will serve them throughout their lives.

Modeling these self-soothing techniques is crucial. When children see you practicing breathing and visualization, they are more likely to adopt these habits themselves. This shared practice creates a supportive environment where emotional regulation becomes a family affair. Integrating these techniques into daily routines, such as before bedtime or during morning preparation, establishes a sense of normalcy around emotional health. This routine not only prepares them for the day ahead but also promotes a calming ritual that can ease them into restful sleep at night.

Building these habits early is vital. When children learn to use breathing and visualization as go-to strategies in stressful moments, they gain a sense of agency over their emotions. This proactive approach to emotional well-being helps them navigate life's ups and downs with greater ease. By investing time in teaching and practicing these techniques, you are laying the foundation for a lifetime of resilience and emotional intelligence. Embrace the power of breathing and visualization and watch as your children flourish in their ability to manage stress and embrace life's challenges with grace.

Problem-Solving Dialogues

When a child encounters a challenge, whether it's a conflict with a friend or the fear of failing, the most effective response is to engage them in a calm and constructive dialogue. This approach not only honors their feelings but also empowers them to navigate their own difficulties, instilling a sense of agency that is crucial for their development.

Consider framing the challenge as a solvable puzzle rather than an insurmountable obstacle. By asking questions like, "How might we handle this?" or "What's one step we can take?" you invite the child to think critically and creatively. This dialogue encourages them to explore various solutions, reinforcing the Stoic belief that while we cannot control external events, we can control our responses to them. Every challenge they face is an opportunity for growth, teaching them that resilience and adaptability are vital skills.

Encouraging the child to weigh the pros and cons of different solutions not only deepens their understanding of the situation but also aligns with the Stoic practice of rational deliberation. It's essential for them to see that every decision carries consequences, and by thoughtfully considering these, they can make informed choices. This method teaches them that in life, clarity of thought can illuminate the path forward, even in the darkest moments.

This collaborative stance does more than guide them through immediate problems; it fosters a sense of independence. They learn to trust their judgment while knowing that your support is a steady presence in their lives. In doing so, you embody the Stoic ideal of being a mentor who remains calm in the face of adversity, demonstrating that while challenges are inevitable, they are also surmountable with patience and reason.

By nurturing this mindset, you equip the child with tools that extend beyond the present challenge. They will carry these lessons into future conflicts and fears, viewing them through the lens of rationality and resilience. In essence, you are not just helping them solve a problem; you are nurturing a lifelong skill set that empowers them to approach life's uncertainties with confidence and composure.

Modeling Healthy Expression of Emotions

Modeling healthy expression of emotions is not merely a beneficial practice; it is a fundamental necessity for the emotional development of children. When frustration or overwhelm arises, instead of succumbing to impulsive reactions, showing children how to acknowledge these feelings without losing composure fosters resilience and emotional intelligence.

By pausing and taking a breath, you embody the stoic principle of self-control, demonstrating that while emotions are natural, they do not dictate one's actions. This practice of mindfulness teaches children that it is acceptable to feel overwhelmed, but it is crucial to manage those feelings constructively. When they observe you navigating emotions thoughtfully, they learn to replicate that behavior, equipping them with invaluable skills for their own emotional journeys.

When you communicate your feelings respectfully, even when upset, you model effective conflict resolution. This is vital in a world where misunderstandings and disagreements are inevitable. Apologizing for moments when you may have snapped or raised your voice reinforces the idea of accountability. It shows children that everyone makes mistakes and that taking responsibility is a sign of strength, not weakness.

Moreover, it is essential to convey that emotional health does not equate to never experiencing negative emotions. Instead, it revolves around the ability to process these feelings in a constructive manner. By consistently demonstrating restraint and honesty, you set a powerful example. Your children will likely imitate this behavior, internalizing the importance of handling emotions with grace and integrity.

In essence, the way you manage your emotions in front of your children can profoundly shape their understanding of emotional health. By modeling these behaviors, you are not just teaching them how to respond to their own emotions; you are cultivating a generation that values self-awareness, accountability, and respectful communication. This foundation will serve them well throughout their lives, guiding them in their personal and interpersonal challenges.

Encouraging Self-Compassion

Encouraging self-compassion in children is essential for their emotional development and resilience. It's important to remind them that everyone makes mistakes or has tough days; this is a universal experience that fosters connection and understanding. By acknowledging that setbacks are part of life, we can help children to view their challenges as opportunities for growth rather than as failures.

Fostering kindness toward oneself is crucial. Teach children that it's perfectly okay to feel disappointed when things don't go as planned, but emphasize that they shouldn't be harsh on themselves. This gentle approach allows them to process their feelings without self-criticism. It creates a safe space for self-reflection, where they can learn to accept their imperfections and recognize that they are worthy of kindness, especially from themselves.

Celebrating the effort of trying, regardless of the outcome, is a pivotal lesson. By praising their attempts rather than just the results, we instill a growth mindset. Children begin to understand that success is not solely defined by immediate achievement but by the courage to try and the persistence to keep going. This shift in perspective encourages them to embrace challenges and take risks without the fear of failure.

In Stoic philosophy, the idea that we are all "works in progress" Strikes a chord in the context of self-compassion. It underscores the notion that personal growth is a journey filled with ups and downs. This understanding empowers children to be patient with themselves, recognizing that improvement takes time and that each experience contributes to their development.

Over time, as children practice self-compassion, they learn to bounce back more quickly from disappointments and setbacks. This resilience is fortified by a sense of inner kindness, which becomes a powerful tool in navigating life's challenges. Encouraging self-compassion not only helps them cope with difficulties but also fosters a more positive and compassionate outlook on themselves and others.

Supporting Children Through Challenges
Allowing "Safe Failures"

In the realm of parenting, the delicate balance between guidance and overprotection emerges as a profound philosophical inquiry, particularly when viewed through the lens of Stoicism. The Stoics held that adversity is not merely an obstacle but a catalyst for personal growth and virtue. In this spirit, allowing children to encounter "safe failures" becomes a crucial aspect of their development.

The Stoic notion of resilience aligns closely with the idea that facing difficulties fortifies one's character. By permitting children to navigate challenges, such as managing school projects or budgeting their allowance, we create opportunities for them to experience the natural consequences of their actions. This practice mirrors the Stoic understanding that external events are beyond our control, while our responses to those events are within our power. In essence, these small failures serve as a training ground for future resilience, teaching children that setbacks are not the end but rather stepping stones on the path to wisdom.

Furthermore, Stoicism emphasizes the importance of accountability. As children take ownership of their decisions, they cultivate a sense of autonomy. This process is not devoid of parental support; instead, it thrives on the careful balance of offering advice while allowing children to make choices. The Stoics would argue that true wisdom arises not from avoidance of difficulties but from grappling with them head-on. Each safe failure illuminates the way forward, guiding children to refine their emotional responses and practical skills, akin to the Stoic practice of reflecting on one's experiences to foster personal growth.

The philosophical underpinning of these safe failures can also be found in the Stoic concept of amor fati, or love of fate. By embracing challenges as essential components of life, children learn to appreciate the inherent value in their struggles. Each moment of disappointment becomes a lesson, each misstep a chance to cultivate virtues such as patience, perseverance, and humility.

Supporting children through challenges by allowing safe failures corresponds with Stoic principles, fostering resilience, accountability, and emotional growth. By guiding them through the trials of life, while allowing them the space to learn from their experiences, we equip them not only to face future adversities but to thrive amidst them. Each safe failure is, therefore, not just a setback, but a vital stepping stone toward a more resilient and virtuous character.

Constructive Conversations After Setbacks

When setbacks occur, the immediate response may be to react with frustration or disappointment, but a more fruitful approach lies in engaging in constructive conversations. Embracing stoic principles, we recognize that while we cannot control external events, we can control our reactions and the way we guide others through their emotions. Instead of delivering knee-jerk lectures that may stifle reflection and growth, we should encourage honest contemplation.

Ask questions like, "What did you learn?" or "What do you think you'll do next time?" These inquiries not only promote self-reflection but also empower individuals to take ownership of their experiences. In the spirit of stoicism, we understand that each setback is an opportunity for growth. A calm debrief allows us to cultivate confidence, reinforcing the belief that challenges are not obstacles but stepping stones to greater resilience.

It is essential to validate feelings. Acknowledge that disappointment is a natural human response; "It's okay to be upset." This validation fosters an environment where individuals feel safe to express their emotions. However, as stoics, we must gently guide them toward a mindset centered on growth. By shifting the focus from what went wrong to how they can improve, we instill a sense of agency and hope.

Cementing the idea that resilience is forged in the aftermath of adversity is crucial. Every challenge provides a lesson that contributes to personal development. In these moments of reflection, we nurture a mindset that views setbacks not as failures, but as integral parts of the journey toward success. By fostering constructive conversations after setbacks, we cultivate resilience and prepare ourselves and others to face future challenges with confidence and grace.

Providing Emotional Safety Nets

Children thrive when they know they can confide in you without the fear of severe judgment or ridicule. This emotional safety net is crucial for their development and well-being. By embodying the principles of Stoicism, we can create an environment where children feel secure enough to express their frustrations and fears openly. Listening attentively, giving them the floor to articulate their feelings, builds trust and demonstrates that their thoughts and emotions are valued.

It is essential to reassure them that needing help or feeling vulnerable is not a sign of weakness but rather an opportunity for growth. Embracing our vulnerabilities is a key tenet of Stoicism; it allows us to confront our challenges with courage and resilience. When children understand that it is acceptable to seek assistance, they learn that strength lies in recognizing their limitations and reaching out for support.

While it is important to offer guidance, we must also empower children to own their journey. This balance nurtures self-reliance, allowing them to develop their internal strength while still feeling the supportive presence of their parents. Stoicism teaches us that true strength is not just about personal fortitude but also about being part of a virtuous community. By fostering both safety and autonomy in our children, we echo this Stoic principle, helping them to build their character and navigate the complexities of life with confidence.

In doing so, we cultivate an environment where children can flourish, knowing they have a strong foundation of emotional support. It is through this lens of Stoicism that we can guide them, encouraging them to face the world with a resilient spirit and a deep sense of self-awareness.

Learning from Role Models and Stories

Throughout history, we have been gifted with remarkable figures who have triumphed over adversity, showcasing the power of resilience. Consider the Stoics, such as Epictetus and Marcus Aurelius. They endured personal hardships—Epictetus was born a slave, and Aurelius faced the weight of leadership during tumultuous times. Yet, they taught us that our responses to challenges define us, not the challenges themselves. Their philosophies encourage us to cultivate inner strength and to confront life's trials with a calm and unwavering spirit.

Hercules and the Hydra

Hercules, in one of his legendary labors, confronted the formidable Lernaean Hydra—a serpent-like monster with multiple heads. Each time he severed one, two more would grow in its place. Understanding that brute force alone would not lead to victory, Hercules adapted his strategy, cauterizing each neck stump with fire to prevent new heads from sprouting. By merging strength with clever tactics, he ultimately triumphed over the Hydra. For parents, the challenges their children face can feel just as daunting and relentless—solving one meltdown or issue only for new struggles to arise. Embracing Stoic resilience reveals that sheer force or rigid rules often fall short without the willingness to adapt. Instead of repeating ineffective methods, we must refine our approaches, employing innovative problem-solving rather than stubborn insistence. Every new "head" presents an opportunity to create and grow, teaching our children—and ourselves—that flexibility combined with determination is far more effective than relentless aggression. This aligns with the Stoic principle that it is not the hardships we encounter but our responses to them that build resilience. By integrating mindful parenting strategies with unwavering commitment, we can conquer recurring challenges, just as Hercules outsmarted the Hydra.

Fictional characters also serve as powerful embodiments of resilience. Harry Potter, for instance, faces relentless obstacles—from the loss of his parents to the constant threat of Voldemort. Yet, he persists, demonstrating not only bravery but also the importance of friendship and loyalty. Each setback he encounters only strengthens his resolve and belief in himself. Through his journey, readers learn that perseverance, coupled with self-belief, can lead to triumph even in the darkest of times.

These role models, both real and fictional, exemplify essential qualities: patience, courage, and self-belief. They teach us that setbacks are not the end but rather stepping stones toward our goals. When children engage with these stories, they internalize powerful messages about resilience. They see that challenges are universal and that they are not alone in their struggles.

Identifying with resilient figures allows children to envision their own potential for overcoming difficulties. By seeing how others have faced and conquered adversity, they are inspired to cultivate similar traits within themselves. This connection ignites a spark of motivation, encouraging them to approach their challenges with the same tenacity as their heroes. Ultimately, the stories we share about resilience, whether from history or fiction, become invaluable tools in shaping the character and determination of the next generation.

Recognizing the Right Time to Intervene

The essence of stoic philosophy teaches us the importance of discernment in our actions. It is crucial to understand that while fostering resilience in children through problem-solving is vital, there are moments when intervention is not just warranted, but necessary. When children face stressors that threaten to overwhelm them—such as bullying or persistent anxiety—stepping in proactively becomes a fundamental responsibility.

Stoicism does not advocate for emotional indifference or a hands-off approach. Instead, it emphasizes the importance of wisdom in our responses to challenges. When children encounter significant hurdles, guiding them through these heavier challenges is essential. A stoic mindset encourages us to acknowledge our limitations and the limitations of those we care for. It teaches us that true strength lies in recognizing when a situation demands more than what we can offer alone.

In instances where problems escalate beyond our expertise, seeking professional help—be it therapy or counseling—should be viewed as a courageous and wise decision. Intervening in such cases is not a sign of failure or weakness; it is an acknowledgment that resilience can also manifest as the willingness to ask for help. This act of seeking assistance reinforces the understanding that life's challenges can sometimes be too great to face in isolation.

By modeling this behavior, we impart a profound lesson to our children: resilience does not equate to enduring hardship alone. Rather, it encompasses the ability to recognize when to reach out for support. In doing so, we prepare them not only to confront challenges but also to appreciate the strength found in community and collaboration. Embracing this stoic principle will empower them to navigate their futures with both fortitude and wisdom.

Integrating Resilience into Family Culture
Open Dialogue About Emotions and Challenges

Integrating resilience into family culture begins with fostering an environment where open dialogue about emotions and challenges is not just welcomed but encouraged. The Stoic philosophy teaches us the importance of confronting reality as it is, acknowledging our emotions, and understanding that setbacks are an integral part of life's journey. By making resilience a common topic of discussion, particularly around the dinner table, families can cultivate a culture that embraces vulnerability and strength.

Encouraging family members to share their daily ups and downs allows everyone to engage in a collective experience of life's ebbs and flows. These conversations transform the dinner table into a safe haven for expression and learning. By openly discussing challenges, each member learns from the experiences of others, gaining insights into different ways of approaching adversity. This practice not only normalizes the concept of facing obstacles but also fosters a sense of belonging and support within the family unit.

When children hear their parents and siblings openly discuss setbacks, they begin to understand that struggle is a universal experience, not a personal failure. Celebrating learning moments is crucial; when a family member shares how they approached a setback, it emphasizes that resilience is not about avoiding difficulties but rather about how we respond to them. This perspective nurtures empathy in children, allowing them to appreciate the struggles of others and, in turn, gain confidence in expressing their own challenges.

Collective reflection on these experiences cements resilience as a shared family value. It transforms individual struggles into communal learning opportunities. By viewing challenges through the lens of growth, families can cultivate a mindset that sees obstacles as stepping stones rather than roadblocks. This Stoic approach not only strengthens familial bonds but also equips each member with the tools necessary to face life's uncertainties with courage and grace.

In this nurturing environment, resilience becomes a cornerstone of family culture. Children learn to navigate their emotions and develop a profound understanding of their own capabilities. They grow up knowing that while they cannot control external circumstances, they can control their responses to them. As a result, they emerge as resilient individuals, ready to tackle life's challenges with the wisdom and strength instilled by their family culture. Embracing this practice not only enhances individual growth but ultimately fortifies the family as a whole, creating a legacy of resilience that can be passed down through generations.

Establish Rituals That Promote Growth

Establishing rituals that promote growth is not merely a suggestion; it is a philosophical imperative that aligns with our understanding of human development and the cultivation of resilience. In a world rife with distractions and uncertainties, these rituals serve as anchors, grounding individuals and families in the pursuit of meaningful existence.

Creating consistent reflection times, such as weekly family meetings or dedicated journaling sessions, fosters a culture of introspection and mindfulness. In these moments, individuals are invited to delve deep into their experiences, unraveling the complexities of their thoughts and emotions. This practice not only nurtures self-awareness but also cultivates a collective understanding within the family unit. By sharing reflections, family members learn to appreciate diverse perspectives, reinforcing the notion that every voice matters and that growth often emerges from the interplay of different experiences.

Encouraging gratitude practices shifts focus from scarcity to abundance. When families dedicate time to acknowledge what went well, they reinforce a mindset that recognizes the positive amid the chaos. This practice is not about ignoring challenges; rather, it invites individuals to appreciate how obstacles can serve as catalysts for growth. By highlighting moments of success and resilience, family members learn to embrace their journey, understanding that every setback carries the potential for transformation.

Celebrating small personal victories is essential in nurturing a growth-oriented mindset. Each step taken to overcome a fear, improve a skill, or resolve a conflict deserves recognition. These celebrations, no matter how minor they may seem, reinforce the idea that progress is a journey composed of many small strides. In doing so, families create an environment where effort is valued, and individuals are empowered to pursue their aspirations without the paralyzing fear of failure.

Rituals provide a tangible structure to the intangible concepts of perseverance and self-improvement. They transform abstract ideals into actionable practices, embedding resilience into the very fabric of family life. When these habits are consistently enacted, they become ingrained, turning resilience from a fleeting concept into a permanent characteristic of the family dynamic.

By establishing rituals that promote growth, families not only enhance their collective strength but also create a legacy of resilience that can be passed down through generations. In a society that often emphasizes immediate gratification, these rituals remind us that true growth is often a gradual process, nurtured by reflection, gratitude, and celebration. Thus, we must embrace the power of these practices, recognizing their potential to transform lives and cultivate a more resilient future.

Model Continuous Learning

Modeling continuous learning is not merely a pedagogical approach; it embodies a profound philosophical principle that is grounded in the essence of human existence. When we openly share our new interests and goals with children, we reinforce the idea that learning is a lifelong journey. This transparency allows them to witness our struggles and triumphs, illuminating the path of resilience that is vital for personal growth.

Philosophically, this aligns with the Stoic ideals of lifelong self-improvement, where the cultivation of virtue and wisdom is a continuous endeavor. By navigating hurdles in front of our children, we illustrate that setbacks are not failures but rather invaluable opportunities for growth. Each mistake we disclose becomes a lesson, an invitation for them to embrace their own imperfections and view challenges as stepping stones rather than roadblocks.

When children observe our determination and commitment to learning, they internalize the belief that resilience is not a trait reserved for the occasional moment of crisis, but a skill that can be honed throughout life. This understanding fosters a mindset that values persistence, adaptability, and the courage to confront the unknown. They learn that emotional resilience is an ongoing process, one that requires patience and practice.

In this context, we not only teach children the importance of being lifelong learners but also empower them to cultivate their own resilience. It encourages them to adopt a proactive stance towards their challenges, realizing that every experience—be it a success or a failure—contributes to their growth. By modeling this behavior, we instill in them a belief in their capacity to navigate life's complexities with grace and fortitude, ensuring they carry these valuable lessons with them as they grow.

Encourage Positive Peer Connections

Encouraging positive peer connections is not merely an enhancement to a child's life; it is essential for their emotional resilience and overall development. Stoic philosophy teaches us that the only things within our control are our thoughts and actions. By fostering healthy friendships and group activities, we are equipping children with the tools they need to navigate life's inevitable challenges with strength and clarity.

It is crucial for children to discern supportive friendships from those that erode their confidence. A wise approach is to guide them in recognizing the qualities of true friendship—trust, respect, and encouragement. These attributes are vital, as they create an environment where a child feels safe to express themselves and face challenges head-on. In contrast, relationships that undermine self-esteem can lead to a cycle of negativity, which Stoicism warns us to avoid.

Encouraging involvement in clubs, sports, or art programs provides children with opportunities to engage in activities that challenge them, all while nurturing supportive environments. Such experiences not only enhance their skills but also cultivate a sense of belonging and teamwork. Within these groups, children learn the value of collaboration and mutual support, which are cornerstones of resilience. They develop the ability to face adversity together, reinforcing the Stoic belief that we are stronger in community.

Furthermore, peer support networks complement parental guidance by introducing diverse perspectives on coping strategies. Children learn from one another, sharing experiences that can illuminate paths through difficulty. This exchange fosters a sense of solidarity and understanding, reminding them that they are not alone in their struggles. As they navigate these relationships, they begin to gravitate towards communities that reinforce their emotional well-being, aligning with the Stoic principle of seeking virtue and wisdom through connection.

In conclusion, by promoting positive peer connections, we empower children to build resilience and emotional fortitude. We instill in them the wisdom to choose friendships that uplift rather than diminish. As they engage in supportive environments, they cultivate not only their individual strengths but also a deeper understanding of the interconnectedness of human experience. In this way, we embody the essence of Stoicism, teaching them to find strength in both their own character and the communities they choose to embrace.

Revisiting Progress and Evolving Goals

Revisiting progress and evolving goals in the context of a child's emotional development is not just an option; it is a necessity rooted in the core principles of Stoicism. As parents, we must recognize that our children are not static beings; they are constantly evolving, facing new challenges that demand our attention and adaptation. Stoicism teaches us the importance of self-reflection and the understanding that life is a series of changes and challenges we must navigate with wisdom and virtue.

Firstly, periodically checking in on your child's emotional landscape is essential. This practice does not merely serve to monitor their feelings but embodies a deeper Stoic principle: the importance of self-awareness. Are they feeling more confident, or do they still grapple with anxiety? By fostering an environment where emotions are openly discussed, we empower our children to articulate their feelings, thus enhancing their emotional intelligence. This aligns with the Stoic belief in understanding oneself to navigate external challenges effectively.

As children grow, their emotional resilience shifts significantly. Strategies that worked for a preschooler may not resonate with a teenager facing peer pressure, academic stress, or identity issues. Acknowledging this evolution is crucial. Stoicism teaches us that adaptability is a virtue. By adjusting our approaches to match our child's developmental stage, we demonstrate resilience in our parenting. We must be willing to let go of outdated methods and embrace new strategies that promote growth and understanding. This adaptability not only reflects our commitment to our children's well-being but also models the Stoic ideal of flexibility in the face of change.

Maintaining fluid dialogues with our children is another vital aspect of fostering resilience. Posing questions like, "How are you handling stress these days? Any new concerns?" invites them to share their thoughts and feelings, reinforcing an open line of communication. This practice aligns with the Stoic approach of seeking wisdom through discourse. By engaging our children in meaningful conversations about their emotional experiences, we not only validate their feelings but also guide them towards self-reflection and problem-solving.

Recognizing that resilience is an ongoing process is a fundamental Stoic belief. Just as we celebrate our children's achievements, we must also acknowledge the challenges they face as part of their growth journey. Each setback can be viewed through the lens of Stoicism as an opportunity for development rather than a failure. By celebrating growth—no matter how small—we instill a sense of accomplishment and encourage a mindset that embraces learning from adversity. This perspective reinforces the idea that resilience is not a fixed trait but a skill that can be cultivated over time.

Finally, ensuring that our family's resilience-building efforts remain relevant over time is crucial. Life will present our children with new challenges, and our approaches must evolve accordingly. This adaptability is not only a reflection of our understanding of Stoic principles but also a commitment to fostering a resilient mindset in our children. By continuously revisiting and adjusting our goals, we teach our children the value of perseverance in the face of constant change.

Using Stoic values in the journey of revisiting progress and evolving goals is essential for nurturing resilient children. Through self-awareness, adaptability, open communication, and recognition of resilience as a continuous process, we equip our children with the tools they need to navigate life's inevitable challenges. This commitment to their emotional growth not only strengthens their resilience but also builds a foundation for a fulfilling and purposeful life.

Key Takeaways (Chapter Cheat Sheet)

1. Emotional Resilience is Learned, Not Innate

   ○ Through guided practices, children develop the mindset and skills to bounce back from setbacks.

2. A Growth Mindset Fuels Confidence

   ○ Focusing on effort, curiosity, and incremental improvements transforms failures into valuable lessons.

3. Practical Coping Tools Build Emotional Strength

   ○ Teaching children to label emotions, use calming techniques, and solve problems fosters lasting resilience.

4. Safe Challenges Encourage Self-Reliance

- Letting kids face age-appropriate adversities helps them learn accountability and coping strategies.

5. Make Resilience a Family Endeavor

    - Open discussions, supportive rituals, and mutual learning embed resilience into your household culture.

Reflection Prompts

1. Journaling Exercise

    - Think of a recent disappointment your child experienced. How did you guide them through it? Is there anything you'd do differently to emphasize resilience next time?

2. Family Discussion

    - Share a story from your own childhood about a failure or setback that ultimately helped you grow. Ask your child if they've had a similar experience.

3. Action Step

    - Identify one upcoming challenge your child might face (a test, a competition, a new social situation). Brainstorm together how they can prepare mentally and emotionally, reinforcing a growth mindset.

By actively teaching and modeling emotional resilience, you equip your children with an invaluable life skill—one that transcends academic achievement and social acceptance. In the face of challenges, your child will feel secure in the knowledge that they have the tools to adapt, learn, and thrive.

Six

The Gift of the Present Moment

"*The present moment is the only time over which we have dominion.*"
— Thích Nhất Hạnh

Although Thích Nhất Hạnh was a Buddhist monk rather than a Stoic philosopher, his teachings on mindfulness and living in the present echo many Stoic ideals. Like Marcus Aurelius and Epictetus, he reminds us that our mental energy is best invested in what we can do here and now, rather than ruminating on the past or fearing the future. For parents, this principle carries profound significance: children grow in real time, and the fleeting nature of each stage reminds us that presence is more transformative than striving for an unachievable perfection.

From a psychological perspective, an overemphasis on "getting everything right" can fuel parental stress, perfectionism, and emotional distance. When parents are constantly pressured by future goals—academic success, extracurricular achievements, the "perfect" home environment—they risk missing small, meaningful moments of connection. Mindfulness research shows that being fully present fosters stronger emotional bonds and reduces anxiety. This aligns with Stoic wisdom that urges us to engage with the now, harnessing our attention for what we can truly influence.

In practice, embracing "presence over perfection" means letting go of rigid expectations and immersing ourselves in everyday interactions—listening intently when children speak, savoring shared laughter, and calmly addressing conflicts as they arise. It's about guiding rather than micromanaging, tuning into genuine needs instead of external pressures. By training our minds to savor the present, we demonstrate to our children that the richest form of parenting—and indeed, living—unfolds in the moment we're experiencing together.

Understanding the Trap of Perfectionism
How Perfectionism Undermines Authenticity

Perfectionism, while often cloaked in the guise of ambition and high standards, is a subtle yet insidious trap that can undermine our authenticity and the connections we cherish most. It creates an emotional distance that not only affects parents but also ripples through to children, stunting their development and emotional well-being. When parents fixate on achieving unrealistic standards, they inadvertently shift their focus away from genuine connection, prioritizing the pursuit of ideal outcomes over the nurturing of meaningful relationships.

Children are remarkably perceptive; they can sense the underlying anxiety or disappointment their parents experience when the relentless quest for perfection takes precedence. This tension breeds an environment steeped in fear—fear of making mistakes, fear of not measuring up, and ultimately, fear of being themselves. In this atmosphere, children may begin to equate their self-worth with external validation, measuring their value by grades, behavior, or appearances rather than their intrinsic qualities. The Stoics remind us that chasing external ideals is a fruitless endeavor. True growth and joy reside not in the perfection of our circumstances but in our internal responses to the inevitable flow of life, with all its imperfections.

Moreover, the emphasis on maintaining a perfect facade—whether in academics, behavior, or household management—distracts us from what truly matters: nurturing emotional bonds and fostering a loving, supportive environment. The relentless pursuit of perfection can lead to a cycle where stress becomes the norm, and fulfillment remains elusive. Over time, this perpetual striving for an ideal can erode the very fabric of our relationships, leaving us feeling isolated and disconnected.

In contrast, embracing the present moment allows us to relinquish the burdens of perfectionism. It encourages us to appreciate the beauty of our imperfections and to engage with our loved ones authentically. By focusing on what is real and immediate, we cultivate resilience and foster deeper connections. Stoic philosophy teaches us to accept what we cannot control and to focus on our actions and responses. This shift in perspective liberates us from the shackles of perfectionism, enabling us to find joy in the journey rather than in an unattainable destination. In doing so, we not only enhance our own well-being but also create a nurturing environment where our children can thrive without the weight of unrealistic expectations.

Recognizing External Pressure

The relentless tide of societal expectations, magnified by the pervasive influence of social media and peer comparisons, creates an environment in which the pursuit of perfection becomes not just a goal but an obsession. In a world where every achievement is broadcast and scrutinized, parents often succumb to the pressure of measuring their worth against the accomplishments of others. This leads to a perilous path where the unique journey of their child is overshadowed by a misguided desire to conform to external standards.

Philosophically, we must turn to the teachings of Stoicism, which emphasize "indifference to externals." This principle asserts that our peace of mind and values should not be contingent upon the opinions or actions of others. In recognizing that societal pressures are mere illusions, parents can liberate themselves from the shackles of comparison. The Stoics remind us that true virtue lies in understanding and accepting what is within our control—our thoughts, intentions, and responses—rather than being swayed by the ephemeral judgments of the outside world.

By consciously identifying and acknowledging these external influences, parents reclaim the agency to define success according to their own values and the unique needs of their children. This shift in perspective is not merely an act of rebellion against societal norms but a profound act of self-awareness and responsibility. It fosters a nurturing environment where children can flourish, unencumbered by the weight of unrealistic expectations.

Over time, the practice of filtering out this external noise cultivates a more authentic and tranquil approach to daily life. As parents learn to prioritize their values over societal pressures, they create a space where their children can explore their individuality without the fear of judgment. This is not a call to abandon ambition or achievement, but rather an invitation to pursue goals that resonate with one's true self, free from the distortions of comparison.

In embracing this Stoic philosophy, parents can find peace and clarity in their parenting journey, allowing their children to thrive as unique individuals. Ultimately, it is through this recognition of external pressures and the conscious choice to rise above them that parents can foster genuine success and fulfillment within their families.

The Emotional Costs of Over-Scheduling

The relentless pursuit of achievement in children's lives, driven by a perfectionist mindset to provide every possible advantage, leads to a detrimental emotional cost that must be reconsidered. Over-scheduling not only fills calendars with endless activities but also erodes the fundamental aspects of childhood—free play, family time, and the essential moments of introspection that nurture emotional well-being.

In the spirit of Stoic philosophy, we must remind ourselves that true contentment does not arise from a packed schedule but from the quality of our experiences. The Stoics teach us the importance of moderation and balance, recognizing that time is a finite resource. Each hour filled with structured activities is an hour taken away from the simple joys of life, the quiet moments of reflection, and the creative pursuits that allow our children to explore their identities.

When we prioritize busyness over presence, we rob our children of the opportunity to savor the moment. The beauty of life often resides in the unplanned and the spontaneous. By scaling back on the constant hustle, we open the door to richer, more meaningful experiences that foster genuine connections and emotional growth.

Encouraging a lifestyle that embraces simplicity and intentionality invites both parents and children to rediscover the art of being rather than doing. It allows them to engage with the world in a way that nurtures creativity and the ability to reflect. The Stoics remind us that tranquility and joy come not from chasing after every potential advantage but from appreciating what we have and finding balance in our lives.

In this light, let us advocate for a shift away from the overwhelming demands of over-scheduling towards a more harmonious existence. Embrace the power of moderation, and allow your family the gift of time—a precious resource that, when cherished, can lead to a richer, more fulfilling life.

When "Good Enough" Is Actually Better

Embracing the concept of "good enough" allows for a richer, more fulfilling experience in life, especially in the developmental stages of childhood. The idea that imperfections can bring value resonates deeply with philosophical ideologies that advocate for acceptance, resilience, and the celebration of the process over the product.

When we allow for messiness in art projects or the occasional clutter of a living room, we create an environment where exploration and creativity flourish. This aligns with the Stoic philosophy, which teaches us to focus on what lies within our control—our efforts and attitudes—rather than striving for an unattainable perfection. In a world that often emphasizes flawless outcomes, children exposed to the notion that "good enough" is acceptable learn to appreciate the journey of learning itself. They understand that the act of trying and experimenting is more valuable than the end result, fostering an intrinsic motivation that is critical for personal growth.

This acceptance of imperfection nurtures resilience. Children learn that failure is not an endpoint but a stepping stone to success. They become accustomed to trial and error, understanding that mistakes are merely opportunities for learning and growth. As they engage in messy, unrefined activities, they develop a sense of confidence in their ability to navigate challenges. This confidence is not rooted in a superficial sense of achievement but rather in the authentic understanding that they can adapt, learn, and improve through experience.

Furthermore, a home that prioritizes sincerity and authenticity over perfection cultivates an atmosphere rich in creativity and genuine connection. Laughter, exploration, and shared experiences replace the anxiety of maintaining a pristine environment. In such spaces, children are encouraged to express themselves freely, resulting in a vibrant tapestry of ideas and interactions that contribute to their emotional and social development.

The philosophy of valuing the process over the product is not merely a practical approach to parenting; it reflects a deeper understanding of human growth. It recognizes that self-esteem built on the foundation of genuine effort, creativity, and exploration is far more enduring than that which stems from mere accolades or polished results. As children grow in these nurturing environments, they carry forward the belief that their worth is not determined by perfection but by their willingness to engage fully with life's myriad experiences.

In conclusion, embracing imperfection and the notion of "good enough" is not just a parenting strategy; it is a profound philosophical stance that fosters resilience, creativity, and genuine self-esteem. By allowing children the freedom to explore, fail, and learn, we equip them with the tools necessary to navigate an imperfect world with confidence and joy.

Perfectionism's Impact on Mental Health.

Perfectionism, often heralded as a virtue, can become a formidable adversary to mental health, fostering anxiety and burnout in both parents and children. Research indicates that high parental perfectionism does not merely affect the individual; it creates an environment where children internalize these unrealistic standards, leading to a cycle of stress that is difficult to escape. This relentless pursuit of perfection can overshadow essential aspects of life like rest, self-care, and joyful spontaneity. It is crucial to recognize that true fulfillment lies not in the unattainable ideal of perfection but in the acceptance of our inherent imperfections.

The Stoics understood that striving for absolute control in an ever-changing world is an exercise in futility. **Voltaire** famously remarked, *"The perfect is the enemy of the good."* He invites us to reconsider our approach to parenting and personal expectations. Rather than attempting to craft a flawless environment or raise a flawless child, we must learn to adapt gracefully to the inevitable challenges that arise. Embracing the Stoic principle of focusing on what is within our control allows us to prioritize emotional well-being over perfectionist ideals.

Recognizing the impact of perfectionism is the crucial first step toward transforming our parenting approach to be more mindful and present. Viktor Frankl, a renowned psychiatrist and Holocaust survivor, powerfully reminds us, "when we can no longer alter a situation, we must rise to the challenge of changing ourselves." To truly overcome perfectionism, we must embrace the profound truth that our worth, as well as that of our children, is not defined by flawless achievements or pristine environments. Instead, it lies in the authenticity of our relationships and the meaningful moments that blossom when we accept our imperfections. Let us choose to prioritize connection over perfection and create a nurturing space where both we and our children can thrive.

As we gradually reduce perfectionistic tendencies, we create space for genuine connection and emotional wellness. Seneca wisely noted, "A good character, when established, is a valuable and lasting possession." By fostering a home environment that values character over perfection, we can nurture resilience and emotional intelligence in ourselves and our children. This shift allows for the cultivation of relationships grounded in understanding and acceptance, rather than fear of failure and disappointment.

In conclusion, the relentless pursuit of perfection is a heavy burden that stifles joy and well-being. By embracing Stoic wisdom and acknowledging the impact of perfectionism on mental health, we can foster a more compassionate, connected, and fulfilling parenting experience. Let us heed the words of Epictetus: "Wealth consists not in having great possessions, but in having few wants." When we shift our focus from perfection to presence, we uncover the richness of life that lies in embracing our imperfections.

Embracing Mindful Presence
The Power of Focused Attention

To cultivate an authentic connection with those around us, particularly our children, we must first embrace the power of focused attention. Active listening, characterized by putting down the phone, maintaining eye contact, and genuinely reflecting on what is said, transcends mere communication; it becomes an act of respect and warmth. This practice forms the bedrock of meaningful relationships, fostering an environment where children feel valued and understood. When children perceive that their thoughts and feelings are genuinely acknowledged, they develop a stronger sense of self-worth and enhanced communication skills, which are essential in navigating the complexities of life.

In our fast-paced world, the temptation to multitask is omnipresent, yet it often leads to a shallow engagement with our loved ones. Mindful presence acts as a counterbalance to this tendency, ensuring that we do not merely hear words while simultaneously planning our next task or worrying about the future. Drawing from Stoic philosophy, this practice channels our energy into the one domain we truly control: our current mindset. By anchoring ourselves in the present moment, we cultivate a sense of tranquility and purpose, allowing us to connect more deeply with our children.

Moreover, the impact of mindful presence extends beyond immediate interactions. As parents model attentive behavior, children absorb these lessons, learning to mirror this approach in their own relationships. This cycle of attentiveness enriches their connections with peers and family alike, creating a ripple effect that fosters empathy and understanding within their social circles. In a world often marred by distraction and superficiality, embracing mindful presence is not just advantageous; it is essential for nurturing future generations equipped with the skills to create meaningful, lasting relationships.

Cultivating Calm Through Breathing and Pauses

Cultivating calm through breathing and pauses is an essential practice that can transform family dynamics. In the heat of the moment, when emotions run high, the ability to take a slow breath before reacting serves as a vital anchor in the present. This technique not only allows family members to regain their composure but also fosters a nurturing environment where understanding can flourish.

Incorporating brief moments of stillness into daily interactions aligns seamlessly with Stoic philosophy, which emphasizes the importance of emotional regulation. Stoics teach us to acknowledge our feelings without allowing them to dictate our actions. By consciously choosing to pause, we embody this principle, recognizing that our emotions are valid but do not have to control us. This practice becomes a powerful tool for families, creating space for reflection rather than impulsive reactions that can lead to conflict.

Children, in particular, are keen observers. When they witness adults taking a moment to breathe and reflect, they learn that it is okay to pause instead of lashing out or shutting down. This modeling of emotional intelligence is invaluable; it empowers them to manage their responses in challenging situations. As they adopt this technique, they cultivate resilience and patience, fundamental virtues that will serve them throughout their lives.

Over time, establishing a home culture centered around mindful breathing promotes cooperative problem-solving. When family members are equipped with the ability to pause, they can approach conflicts with clarity and calmness. This shift in perspective encourages collaboration rather than confrontation, leading to more constructive conversations and stronger relationships.

In a world filled with distractions and pressures, embracing the Stoic approach of cultivating calm through breathing and pauses not only enhances individual well-being but also strengthens familial bonds. By committing to this practice, families can create a sanctuary of peace and understanding, allowing each member to flourish within a supportive and harmonious environment.

Micro-Moments of Connection

Micro-Moments of Connection are the lifeblood of meaningful relationships, emphasizing that presence does not rely on extravagant gestures or meticulously planned quality time. In our fast-paced world, it is the everyday moments—a brief conversation after school, a shared laugh while washing dishes—that truly nurture deeper bonds and cultivate lasting connections.

Philosophical ideologies, particularly from the Stoics, remind us to live fully in each moment, to be alert to the small wonders that surround us. The Stoics believed that life's richness is found in the present, in the fleeting yet meaningful interactions that might otherwise go unnoticed. By embracing these micro-moments, we nurture relationships that transcend the superficiality of achievements and accolades.

Consider the emotional currency that arises from these spontaneous interactions. When a child engages in a light-hearted exchange with a parent, they feel valued not for their grades or accomplishments but for their very existence. This recognition lays a foundation of self-worth and security. Over time, these consistent micro-connections accumulate, creating a reservoir of warmth and trust that fortifies the relationship against the inevitable challenges of life.

In a society that often prioritizes the grand and the spectacular, we must advocate for the significance of these small yet profound moments. They are the threads that weave the fabric of our relationships, reminding us that love and connection are not solely built on significant events but are cultivated in the ordinary moments we often take for granted. Embracing the philosophy of presence allows us to transform our daily interactions into opportunities for growth, understanding, and deep emotional connection.

Mindful Routines and Rituals

Mindful routines and rituals embody the Stoic values of presence, reflection, and community. Regular rituals such as a tech-free family dinner or a bedtime gratitude circle serve as essential touchpoints that foster a sense of safety and belonging among family members. Stoicism emphasizes the importance of focusing on what we can control, and by establishing these predictable routines, families create an environment where members can engage meaningfully with one another, free from external distractions.

These rituals also provide a structured opportunity for self-reflection, a core Stoic practice. By discussing the day's highs and lows during family gatherings, individuals can practice the Stoic principles of examining their thoughts and actions. This self-reflection nurtures personal growth and encourages family members to cultivate virtues such as gratitude, resilience, and humility. As they share their experiences, they learn to appreciate the transient nature of both joy and sorrow, aligning their daily lives with the Stoic understanding that all things are temporary.

Over time, these rituals transform into cherished traditions that offer solace and stability amidst life's inevitable changes. In a world characterized by uncertainty, having a set time for connection reinforces the Stoic belief in the importance of community. Family members come to look forward to these intervals of genuine togetherness, recognizing them as moments to practice empathy and support for one another.

Ultimately, mindful routines and rituals grounded in Stoic values not only enhance the individual's capacity for self-reflection but also strengthen familial bonds. They create a nurturing environment where every member can feel secure and valued, encouraging a collective journey toward personal and communal growth.

Balancing Screen Time and Real Interaction

In today's world, where modern technology pervades every aspect of our lives, it is essential to acknowledge the philosophical values that guide our relationship with screens. The fragmentation of attention caused by notifications, endless feeds, and digital entertainment is not merely a nuisance; it is a fundamental challenge to our ability to engage in meaningful interactions. By setting boundaries on screen usage, families can reclaim precious moments like mealtimes and conversations, which are vital for nurturing relationships and building a sense of community.

Drawing upon Stoic principles, we are reminded of the importance of using tools deliberately, rather than allowing them to dominate our minds and lives. The Stoics teach us that true power lies in our ability to control our responses to external stimuli. By consciously limiting screen time, we reinforce the idea that technology is a tool meant to serve us, not a master to which we must submit. This deliberate approach encourages mindfulness, allowing us to focus on what truly matters—our relationships and the world around us.

Furthermore, children learn by observing their parents. When they witness their parents regulating their own screen habits, they internalize healthier boundaries regarding technology. This modeling is crucial in fostering an environment where genuine presence becomes the default mode of family life. Children who grow up in such settings are more likely to establish their own healthy relationships with technology, leading to a generation that values real interaction over digital distraction.

The long-term benefits of reduced screen interference extend beyond individual families. As we cultivate environments rich in authentic connection, we contribute to a societal shift that prioritizes meaningful interactions. In a world increasingly dominated by screens, choosing to engage with each other rather than our devices is a radical act of resistance against the pervasive influence of technology.

To achieve this balance, families must adopt a proactive stance, implementing strategies that promote real interaction. Regular tech-free family meals, designated screen-free times, or engaging in shared activities can help create spaces where conversations thrive, and connections deepen. By prioritizing these moments, we honor the philosophical values that emphasize the importance of presence, community, and the deliberate use of our resources.

In conclusion, the challenge of balancing screen time and real interaction is not merely a logistical issue but a philosophical one. By invoking

Stoic principles and emphasizing the value of genuine presence, we can reclaim our family lives from the distractions of modern technology. It is through our choices that we shape our relationships, and in doing so, we create a legacy of connection for future generations.

Encouraging Child-Led Play and Exploration
The Magic of Unstructured Play

Letting children direct their play fosters creativity, problem-solving, and emotional resilience. In a world where structured activities dominate, the value of unstructured play often goes unnoticed. Stoic philosophy teaches us the importance of focusing on what we can control and accepting what we cannot. By allowing children the freedom to explore their interests without constant adult intervention, we give them a vital opportunity to engage with the world on their terms.

Epictetus said "Freedom is the only worthy goal in life. It is won by disregarding things that lie beyond our control." When children are given the autonomy to choose how they spend their time, they learn to navigate their environment, make decisions, and experience the consequences of their choices. This process is not just about play; it is a fundamental aspect of their development.

Constantly orchestrating activities can stifle a child's imagination, mirroring parental perfectionism. Just as Stoics advise against the pursuit of external validation and the need for control, parents should refrain from micromanaging their children's experiences. In doing so, we inadvertently teach them that their ideas and interests are not as valuable as the structured activities we provide. Instead, children should be encouraged to follow their curiosities, experiment with their ideas, and develop their identities through play.

Stoic serenity values freedom within reason—child-led play is a microcosm of self-directed growth. The lessons learned during unstructured playtime extend beyond the moment; they instill a sense of self-efficacy and resilience. As children navigate challenges in their imaginative worlds, they develop problem-solving skills that will serve them throughout their lives. This autonomy fosters an environment where creativity thrives, and children learn that their perspectives matter.

Over time, children learn to trust their own ideas and cultivate independent interests. This trust is foundational to their development and self-esteem. When parents step back and allow for exploration, they empower their children to embrace their unique paths. The spontaneity of child-led play can lead to unexpected moments of joy and discovery, not just for the child but for the parent as well.

Parents discover joy in witnessing spontaneous, creative exploration unfold. The laughter, the unexpected outcomes, and the sheer delight of imaginative play create a shared experience that strengthens the parent-child bond. By stepping back, parents not only nurture their child's growth but also allow themselves to revel in the beauty of childhood's fleeting moments.

Stoic principles of fostering an environment where children can grow into independent, resilient individuals, encapsulates the ideology of child-led play. By relinquishing control and encouraging exploration, we honor the essence of childhood and cultivate a generation equipped to navigate the complexities of life with creativity and confidence.

Letting Go of Outcome-Based Pressure

Letting go of outcome-based pressure is essential for fostering a healthy environment for children's development. When we resist the urge to measure success in children's play by neatness, speed, or the perfection of a final product, we unlock a powerful avenue for genuine exploration and learning. Children are naturally curious, and when they engage in play without the looming expectation of external validation, they are free to discover, experiment, and innovate. This process-oriented approach promotes a love for learning that is intrinsic rather than extrinsic.

In a society that often equates achievement with accolades, we must remind ourselves—especially in the context of childhood play—that the journey is far more significant than the destination. Adopting a Stoic perspective, we recognize that virtue is found in the act of engaging with the process itself. The focus shifts from striving for perfection to embracing the act of creation, where the experience of play becomes a valuable lesson in itself. This perspective not only enriches a child's understanding but also cultivates a mindset that values effort over outcome.

Furthermore, when children engage wholeheartedly in tasks without the pressure of producing a specific result, they learn resilience. The reality of play is that outcomes can vary significantly; the messy, imperfect nature of creativity is a fundamental aspect of growth. By allowing children to experience failure or unexpected results, we equip them with the tools necessary to face larger challenges in life. They learn that setbacks are not a reflection of their worth or abilities, but rather a natural part of any meaningful endeavor.

Over time, this approach instills a profound sense of confidence. Children who are encouraged to explore without fear of judgment develop a robust self-esteem that prepares them for future challenges—both in academics and in life. They become more adaptable, willing to take risks, and resilient in the face of adversity. As we shift our focus from outcome to process, we not only enhance the quality of play but also lay a strong foundation for lifelong learning and personal growth. Embracing this philosophy is not merely beneficial; it is essential for nurturing the next generation's ability to thrive in an ever-changing world.

Learning Through Natural Consequences

When we consider the philosophical value of experiential wisdom, it becomes evident that allowing children to navigate small obstacles on their own is not merely an option but a necessity for their development. Instead of jumping in to solve every minor frustration or disagreement, parents should embrace the idea that natural consequences can serve as powerful teachers. When a child learns that a toy breaks because it was used roughly, they gain a deeper understanding of responsibility that no lecture could impart. This direct experience engages them in a way that words alone cannot.

Stoicism, with its emphasis on learning through experience, underscores the importance of testing reality and adapting accordingly. By stepping back—when it is safe to do so—parents empower their children to confront challenges head-on. This process is not just about facing obstacles; it is about developing problem-solving skills and emotional regulation. Children learn to pause, assess situations, and respond rather than react impulsively. This cultivation of self-reliance and resilience is invaluable.

Over time, children who are allowed to experience the natural consequences of their actions begin to realize that they can handle missteps. This realization fosters a sense of independence that is crucial for their overall growth. Instead of viewing mistakes as failures, they come to see them as opportunities for learning and growth. Calm perseverance becomes a natural outcome of this process, equipping them with the tools they need to face life's larger challenges with confidence.

In fostering this environment of learning through natural consequences, we align ourselves with a philosophy that champions the idea that real understanding is forged in the fires of experience. By resisting the urge to intervene at every turn, we open the door for our children to develop into competent, resilient individuals capable of navigating the complexities of life on their own. This approach not only nurtures their independence but also instills a lifelong love of learning, ensuring that they are well-prepared for whatever challenges lie ahead.

Being Present Without Hovering

Being present without hovering is a crucial aspect of parenting that aligns closely with Stoic values. The Stoics believed in the importance of virtue, wisdom, and the cultivation of one's character. When we apply these principles to parenting, we recognize that our role is not to control every aspect of our children's lives but to support their growth within the framework of healthy boundaries.

Emotional support and encouragement are vital, yet they should not translate into micromanagement. Just as the Stoics taught the significance of focusing on what is within our control, we must understand that our children's actions and decisions ultimately belong to them. By resisting the urge to hover over them in every endeavor, we allow them the space to explore, make mistakes, and learn from experiences. This approach fosters resilience, a key Stoic tenet, as children learn to navigate challenges independently.

Children flourish under watchful yet non-invasive guidance. This balance reflects the Stoic ideal of moderation—being present enough to offer reassurance and advice while allowing a child the freedom to exercise their judgment. When parents establish loving boundaries, children feel secure yet empowered. They understand that they are supported, but not suffocated by overbearing oversight. This environment nurtures their confidence and encourages them to think critically, building a foundation for sound decision-making.

Over time, as we practice this balance, children internalize self-confidence, understanding that their parents trust their evolving judgment. This trust is not merely a gift; it is a responsibility that cultivates maturity. By stepping back, we teach them that they are capable of navigating the world, reinforcing the Stoic belief in the power of individual agency and self-governance.

This harmonious dynamic, where parents remain present but not overbearing, aligns with the Stoic view of relationships rooted in respect and understanding. It is a testament to the belief that true love for our children lies not in control, but in the freedom we grant them to grow into their own person. This approach not only honors their autonomy but also strengthens the parent-child relationship, creating a bond built on mutual respect and trust. Embracing this philosophy allows us to foster well-rounded individuals who are equipped to face life's challenges with confidence and grace.

Celebrating the Joy of Discovery

Celebrating the joy of discovery is essential in nurturing not only a child's development but also the bond between parent and child. When children learn something new, like tying their shoelaces or building a block tower, it is imperative that we, as parents, share in their excitement. This celebration becomes a profound moment that goes beyond mere acknowledgment; it is a recognition of their effort and curiosity.

By engaging with genuine curiosity, asking questions, and marveling alongside them, we deepen our connection. This interaction reflects a vital Stoic value: the appreciation for the ordinary wonders of life. Each small triumph—each new skill learned—is worth noticing and celebrating. Stoicism teaches us to find value in the present moment and to recognize that every experience contributes to our growth. For our children, these moments are not trivial; they are pivotal in shaping their understanding of their own capabilities and the world around them.

Over time, as we celebrate their discoveries, children come to sense that their pursuits and achievements matter. This recognition enhances their motivation and self-worth, fostering a resilient spirit that values effort over mere outcomes. In a society often fixated on rigid expectations and external validation, the joy of shared discovery becomes a sanctuary of encouragement, allowing them to explore their interests without fear of judgment.

Furthermore, this joint celebration cements a culture of presence. It cultivates an environment where mutual delight surpasses the constraints of rigid expectations. In doing so, we embody Stoic principles by focusing on what we can control—our reactions and our attitudes—while teaching our children to do the same. We help them understand that the act of learning is a journey, and every step taken is a reason for joy, regardless of the outcome.

In essence, by celebrating the joy of discovery, we not only nurture their growth but also enrich our own lives. This shared experience builds a foundation of trust, love, and mutual respect, allowing both parents and children to flourish. Embracing this Stoic perspective, we can transform ordinary moments into extraordinary celebrations of life's endless possibilities.

Navigating Stressful Moments with Presence
Recognizing Stress Triggers

Recognizing stress triggers is essential for maintaining a calm and composed mindset, especially for parents facing the daily pressures of life. Rushing to appointments, dealing with clutter, or managing work demands can lead to heightened stress levels, which ultimately erodes the tranquility we strive to cultivate. Identifying these triggers early allows parents to implement preventive measures—such as leaving earlier, simplifying routines, or delegating tasks to others.

The wisdom of Stoic philosophy emphasizes the importance of foresight and preparation. As Marcus Aurelius noted, "You have power over your mind—not outside events. Realize this, and you will find strength." This quote speaks directly to the heart of navigating stress: it is not the external pressures that define our state of mind, but our internal responses to those pressures. By recognizing potential difficulties ahead of time, parents can plan accordingly, reducing the likelihood of becoming overwhelmed by unexpected challenges.

Adopting a proactive approach not only helps in minimizing stress but also fosters a mindful presence. When parents prepare for the inevitable stressors of daily life, they are less likely to respond with snap judgments or engage in heated conflicts. This measured response creates a more harmonious environment, where calmness and clarity prevail. Moreover, this practice serves as a powerful lesson for children. They observe how their parents handle stress and learn to prepare for and cope with challenges constructively.

As parents embody the values of Stoicism—accepting what they cannot control while taking responsibility for their responses—they model resilience and composure for their children. This not only strengthens familial bonds but also equips the next generation with vital skills for navigating their own stressful moments. Through this lens, the act of recognizing stress triggers becomes not just a personal endeavor, but a shared journey toward greater emotional intelligence and stability.

Responding Rather Than Reacting

In moments of tension, whether it be a toddler's tantrum or a sibling fight, the importance of responding rather than reacting cannot be overstated. This pause before speaking is not merely a tactical maneuver; it is a deeply philosophical practice rooted in the values of mindfulness and emotional intelligence. By taking a breath, we break the cycle of impulsive, emotion-fueled reactions that often escalate conflicts rather than resolve them.

Stoic teachings emphasize the power of choice in the face of adversity. In the heat of the moment, it is all too easy to let anger dictate our behavior, leading to hasty words and actions that we may later regret. Instead, by choosing to pause, we embody the virtues of patience and empathy. It is an opportunity to reflect on our values and to act in accordance with them, rather than allowing our emotions to take the wheel.

Moreover, this practice has profound implications for our children. When they witness their parents or caregivers maintaining composure amidst chaos, they learn that calmness is not only possible but also a powerful response to conflict. This modeling of thoughtful responses over reactive behaviors fosters an environment where children can develop their own skills in de-escalation. They begin to internalize the notion that emotions do not have to dictate their actions, but rather, they can choose how to respond to any given situation.

Families that embrace this philosophy cultivate a culture of understanding and respect. Thoughtful words and gestures replace heated exchanges, leading to deeper connections and stronger relationships. By prioritizing response over reaction, we teach our children the invaluable lesson that they possess agency in their interactions, empowering them to navigate conflicts with grace and wisdom.

Ultimately, the choice to pause transforms not only individual moments of tension but also the very fabric of family dynamics. It is a commitment to virtue, a pathway to emotional resilience, and a foundation for fostering harmony in the home. In this way, we not only respond to immediate challenges but also shape the character and emotional well-being of the next generation.

Using Grounding Techniques

Zeno's Arrow Paradox

The Greek philosopher Zeno introduced a paradox that reveals a profound truth: an arrow in flight appears motionless at every infinitesimal moment, seeming "at rest" in a precise location. This leads us to question the very nature of motion, suggesting it might be an illusion. While Zeno's paradox engages with abstract reasoning, it powerfully highlights that each instant is complete and self-contained. As parents, we often find ourselves tempted to rush forward—worrying about the future or fixating on past mistakes—while neglecting the immense power of the present moment. When we apply Zeno's arrow paradox through a Stoic lens, we recognize that the only time we truly inhabit is "now." Effective parenting requires us to be fully present; we cannot guide our children well if our thoughts are consumed by tomorrow's anxieties or yesterday's regrets. By anchoring ourselves in the moment—listening intently to a child's story, cherishing a spontaneous hug, or calmly navigating a meltdown—we embody the Stoic principle that genuine influence stems from our present actions. Life may continue its relentless march, but within each fleeting instant lies our chance to engage wholeheartedly, shaping not only our child's experiences but also our own sense of mindful presence.

Grounding techniques, such as naming three things you see, hear, or feel, serve as powerful tools for re-anchoring our minds in the present.

This simple practice aligns perfectly with Stoic values, emphasizing the importance of focusing on what is within our control. By redirecting our attention to our immediate surroundings, we cultivate mindfulness and resilience, crucial traits for navigating life's inevitable challenges.

Teaching children these quick exercises not only empowers them but also instills essential self-soothing skills that they can utilize independently. The Stoics believed in the importance of self-mastery and emotional regulation, and by equipping children with grounding techniques, we are preparing them to face adversity with a steady mind. Just as Marcus Aurelius wrote about the power of our perceptions, these exercises help young minds learn to shift their focus from overwhelming emotions to tangible realities.

Furthermore, the Stoic practice of negative visualization reminds us to prepare for potential setbacks and appreciate our current circumstances. By employing mental resets, we can transform stressful moments into opportunities for growth and emotional regulation. This perspective shift enables us to view challenges not as threats but as occasions for development and strength.

Over time, these grounding habits foster a sense of presence that transcends mere theory. Instead of viewing presence as a lofty ideal, we can recognize it as a practical tool for daily life. By consistently practicing these techniques, we cultivate a mindset that is resilient, focused, and ultimately empowered to handle whatever comes our way. Embracing these Stoic principles through grounding techniques not only enriches our lives but also serves as a beacon of stability for those around us, particularly for the younger generations we aim to guide.

Maintaining Perspective on Small Setbacks

The notion that a spilled drink or a forgotten lunch constitutes a moral failing is not only misguided but fundamentally undermines the very essence of a balanced perspective on life. In the grand tapestry of existence, these minor mishaps are mere threads that contribute to a richer understanding of our humanity. Viewing such occurrences with levity is not just a practical approach; it is a philosophical imperative that fosters resilience and harmony within family dynamics.

Stoicism teaches us that events themselves are neutral, and it is our reactions that shape our experience. To allow frustration to take hold over trivialities is to surrender our power to external circumstances. Instead, embracing humor and patience in the face of these small setbacks not only alleviates tensions but cultivates an environment where emotional intelligence thrives.

Children are acutely observant, and when they witness adults grappling with minor blunders, they learn that mistakes are not catastrophic but rather integral to the human experience. This perspective nurtures a growth mindset, fostering the understanding that each error is an opportunity for learning rather than a cause for shame. As families normalize these slip-ups, they shift from a blame-centric approach to one that prioritizes solutions and collaboration.

The presence of mindfulness during these minor mishaps is crucial. It acts as a bulwark against the potential escalation into larger emotional crises. By addressing these moments with grace and humor, we prevent them from snowballing into greater tensions that can disrupt familial harmony. Therefore, let us champion a philosophy that recognizes the triviality of minor disturbances and instead focus on fostering an atmosphere of understanding, patience, and love. In doing so, we not only enhance our own lives but also provide a valuable lesson in resilience for future generations.

Turning Conflict into Connection

Turning conflict into connection is not merely a desirable outcome; it is an essential skill that can shape our relationships and emotional well-being. After a stressful event, initiating open dialogue with questions like "What happened? How did we feel? What can we learn?" is a powerful way to foster understanding and growth. This reflective presence allows individuals to process their experiences together, analyzing triggers, emotions, and outcomes in a safe and constructive manner.

From a psychological standpoint, engaging in open dialogue after conflict encourages emotional intelligence. Children learn to articulate their feelings, recognize the emotions of others, and develop empathy. This process not only helps them understand the complexities of human interaction but also cultivates a sense of belonging and connection. Rather than viewing conflict as something to be feared or avoided, they come to see it as an opportunity for collaboration and growth, reinforcing the idea that challenges can be faced together.

The Stoic philosophy underscores the importance of virtuous living through understanding and self-reflection. By encouraging a mindset that views conflict as a chance to learn, we align with Stoic principles that advocate for resilience and emotional regulation. Stoics teach us that our responses to external events are within our control. When we approach conflicts with a mindset of inquiry rather than accusation, we embody the Stoic ideal of maintaining composure and rationality in the face of adversity.

Over time, as children internalize these practices, they become adept at resolving problems collaboratively and calmly. This cyclical process of mindful conflict resolution helps establish a foundation of trust and respect, ensuring that each upset becomes a shared learning experience rather than a source of lingering resentment. The ability to turn conflict into connection not only strengthens relationships but also instills lifelong skills in emotional resilience and effective communication.

In essence, the practice of reflective presence in the aftermath of conflict cultivates a culture of understanding and cooperation. By modeling these behaviors, we empower the next generation to navigate their relationships with empathy and wisdom, ultimately enriching their lives and the lives of those around them.

Sustaining Presence as a Family Value
Frequent Check-Ins and Gratitude

Frequent check-ins and expressions of gratitude are not merely practices; they are the very foundation of a thriving family life. In an age where distractions abound, setting aside moments during meals or bedtime to share experiences of presence cultivates a shared awareness that binds family members closer together. Each person recounting a moment when they felt most "present" fosters a sense of belonging and significance, echoing the philosophical tenets of existentialism which emphasize the importance of individual experience and authenticity.

Expressing gratitude for small joys—whether it's a funny joke shared, a helping hand offered, or a calm resolution to a challenge—transforms mundane moments into profound connections. This practice aligns with the teachings of Stoicism, where the act of journaling about positive experiences helps individuals develop a mindset grounded in appreciation. By reflecting on these moments, families not only enhance their emotional resilience but also enrich their collective narrative, reinforcing the idea that life's simplest pleasures are worthy of acknowledgment.

Over time, this daily reflection cultivates a deeper capacity to notice and appreciate life's everyday gifts. It encourages an attitude of mindfulness, allowing family members to engage with their surroundings and each other in a more meaningful way. From a philosophical perspective, this practice aligns with the principles of virtue ethics, which advocate for the cultivation of character through habitual reflection and gratitude. By embedding these values into family routines, we not only strengthen our connections but also instill a legacy of presence and appreciation that can be passed down through generations. In essence, committing to these practices is a profound affirmation of life itself, a testament to the power of human connection, and a celebration of the beauty inherent in our shared experiences.

Setting Realistic Goals Together

Setting realistic goals together is not just a practical approach; it is a transformative philosophical journey that can strengthen family dynamics. By collaboratively planning family objectives, such as improving morning routines or reducing screen time, we can create an environment where each member feels valued and involved. This process encourages families to break down larger aspirations into small, attainable steps, making progress tangible and motivating.

Celebrating incremental wins is crucial in this journey. It shifts the focus from unrealistic perfectionism to acknowledging shared progress, fostering an atmosphere where everyone feels encouraged to contribute. This practice not only nurtures a sense of accomplishment but also reinforces the idea that every small victory matters. By celebrating these moments, families cultivate a positive outlook that emphasizes growth over flawlessness.

Aligning with Stoic principles of moderation, these goals embody a balanced approach to life. Instead of succumbing to all-or-nothing extremes, families learn to appreciate the journey of improvement. This philosophical grounding teaches children valuable lessons about resilience and adaptability. They come to understand that consistent effort is more rewarding than the pursuit of unattainable standards, leading to a healthier mindset.

Over time, the process of setting and achieving realistic goals together fosters deeper connections within the family unit. As members work towards common objectives, they bond over collective achievements, creating a supportive atmosphere that encourages open communication and collaboration. This shared experience not only builds trust but also instills a sense of belonging and unity.

Setting realistic goals together is a powerful strategy that nurtures family relationships while instilling essential life lessons. By embracing moderation, celebrating progress, and fostering a supportive environment, families can navigate challenges together, ultimately leading to a more harmonious and fulfilling life.

Balancing Future Plans and Present Joy

Balancing future plans with present joy is not merely a task; it's an art that requires the wisdom of Stoicism. It is essential to recognize the significance of planning for your child's education and future needs. However, this responsibility must not become a burden that overshadows the joy of the present moment. The Stoics teach us that while we can anticipate the future, we must also ground ourselves in the reality of today.

The future is inherently uncertain, and life is filled with unexpected shifts. By embracing this uncertainty, we cultivate flexibility that allows us to adapt to changing circumstances. Instead of fixating on distant goals, we can appreciate the beauty and richness of the present, fostering a sense of gratitude for what is immediately available. This approach does not negate our aspirations; rather, it enhances our experience of the journey toward those aspirations.

Stoic wisdom encourages us to acknowledge our desires for the future while maintaining an unwavering focus on the present. We can teach our children the value of foresight without sacrificing the joys that exist in the here and now. This balanced perspective is essential for their development, as it allows them to appreciate the fleeting moments of joy while also understanding the importance of planning and preparation.

As children observe their parents navigating the delicate balance between future ambitions and present satisfaction, they internalize these lessons. They learn to cultivate a mindset that values strategic foresight but recognizes that happiness is found in the moments we often take for granted. By modeling this behavior, we equip them with the tools to approach life with resilience and contentment.

So let us embrace the Stoic principle of living fully in the present while responsibly planning for the future. By doing so, we create a harmonious environment where our children can thrive, learning to appreciate life's journey, with all its uncertainties, while cherishing the joy of today.

Modeling Mindful Breaks

Modeling mindful breaks is not merely a practice; it is a profound philosophical commitment to self-awareness and well-being that can transform the lives of children. By demonstrating the importance of stepping away from tasks, whether through a brief walk, a stretch, or a moment of mindful breathing, we instill in children a foundational understanding of self-care. This practice normalizes the idea that taking time for oneself is not a luxury but a necessity, emphasizing that true presence in any task is inherently linked to an awareness of one's energy levels.

In a world that often glorifies productivity at the expense of mental health, teaching children to pace themselves is a revolutionary act. It embodies the philosophical values of balance and moderation, echoing the ancient wisdom of Aristotle, who advocated for the "Golden Mean." By encouraging children to recognize when they are overwhelmed and to step back, we empower them to avoid the pitfalls of burnout. This fosters sustained engagement, allowing them to approach tasks with renewed vigor and clarity rather than fatigue and frustration.

Over time, these mindful breaks can seamlessly integrate into the family's daily routine, creating a culture that prioritizes reflection over relentless activity. This integration is not just beneficial; it is essential in preventing chronic stress. Stress, when left unmanaged, can lead to a cascade of negative effects, stifling creativity and diminishing overall quality of life. By consciously choosing to pause, we teach our children that life is not merely a series of tasks to be completed but an experience to be savored and reflected upon.

Inherent in this practice is the recognition that presence is not a fleeting aspiration but a habit to cultivate. Presence becomes a living, breathing part of family life, a continuous practice rather than a one-time goal. As children observe and mirror this behavior, they learn to navigate their own emotional landscapes with grace and awareness. This philosophical shift towards valuing mindful breaks ultimately cultivates a generation that understands the importance of balance, reflection, and self-care, equipping them with the tools to thrive in an increasingly demanding world.

Celebrating Imperfect Progress

Celebrating imperfect progress is essential for nurturing a resilient family culture grounded in Stoic values. It is inevitable that family members will sometimes revert to over-scheduling or distraction. When these slips occur, it is crucial to approach them with understanding rather than criticism. Recognizing that such moments are part of our shared human experience allows us to maintain an atmosphere of compassion and support.

Renewed efforts to re-center ourselves should be embraced as opportunities for growth. Mindful presence is not a destination but an ongoing practice that requires patience and dedication. Each time we recognize a need to reset, we engage in a powerful act of Stoic resilience. These moments of stumbling should not be viewed as failures; rather, they serve as prompts to realign with our core virtues, reminding us of our commitment to presence and purpose.

As we celebrate these comebacks, we reinforce a narrative of perseverance, acceptance, and growth within our family. The acknowledgment of our collective journey, with its inevitable ups and downs, fosters an environment where everyone feels encouraged to strive for improvement. This shared commitment to presence, despite the bumps along the road, strengthens our bonds and cultivates a deeper understanding of one another.

By embracing imperfect progress, we teach our family members that the path to mindfulness and presence is not linear. Each reset is an opportunity to learn, adapt, and grow together. In doing so, we weave Stoic principles into the fabric of our family culture, instilling resilience and encouraging a lifelong commitment to self-improvement and harmony. Together, we navigate the challenges of life, celebrating not just the achievements, but also the journeys that shape us.

Key Takeaways (Chapter Cheat Sheet)

1. Perfectionism Inhibits Genuine Connection

- Striving for flawless outcomes often overshadows real growth and bonding—embrace process over product.
2. Mindful Presence Cultivates Deeper Bonds

    - Focused attention, calming rituals, and tech boundaries help families engage fully in everyday moments.
3. Child-Led Exploration Encourages Independence

    - Allowing unstructured play and natural consequences fosters creativity, resilience, and self-discovery.
4. Respond, Don't React, in Stressful Moments

    - Brief pauses and grounding techniques can transform chaos into teachable, solution-focused interactions.
5. Presence Is a Lifelong Practice

    - Through consistent reflection, gratitude, and self-awareness, families weave mindful living into daily routines.

Reflection Prompts

1. Journaling Exercise

    - Recall a recent moment when you felt rushed or preoccupied. How might slowing down or focusing intently have altered that experience?
2. Family Discussion

    - Ask each family member to share a simple, meaningful moment from the past few days—a snippet of laughter, a

small kindness, or a calm resolution. How did being "present" enhance it?
3. Action Step

- Choose one daily activity (e.g., breakfast, bedtime story, a quick walk) to practice complete presence—no phones, no multitasking. Notice the difference it makes in mood and connection.

Conclusion

Very little is needed to make a happy life; it is all within yourself, in your way of thinking." — Marcus Aurelius

Marcus Aurelius, both an emperor and a Stoic philosopher, recognized that true contentment does not stem from accumulating possessions or chasing endless goals. He championed the idea that happiness is found in nurturing an inner sense of peace and clarity. In our fast-paced world, this wisdom resonates powerfully as families grapple with relentless advertisements, overflowing to-do lists, and societal pressures to provide every possible advantage. The Stoic principle of simplifying urges us to cut through these external distractions and reconnect with what truly nourishes our souls. Philosophically and psychologically, simplifying means actively removing the noise—whether it's physical clutter, chaotic schedules, or emotional burdens—that hinders our ability to forge meaningful connections.

Research on minimalism and mindfulness shows that a simplified environment reduces stress, allowing individuals to focus on what genuinely matters. This aligns perfectly with the Stoic teaching that emphasizes valuing what lies within our control: our mindset, how we spend our time, and the quality of our relationships. Rather than constantly striving for more, simplifying encourages us to embrace what is sufficient.

For parents, adopting this mindset can dramatically enhance daily life. It transcends merely decluttering play areas or scaling back extracurricular activities—though these actions are certainly beneficial. It embodies a philosophy that prioritizes inner fulfillment over external pressures. By intentionally selecting fewer, more meaningful activities and possessions, parents can teach their children that peace of mind isn't about keeping up with the Joneses; it's about living purposefully. Simplification thus emerges as a fundamental principle that fosters a more serene home environment, strengthens family bonds, and clarifies our path toward the virtues celebrated in Stoic philosophy. I've often found myself reflecting on an ancient piece of wisdom: "Anyone can hold the helm when the sea is calm." But in parenting, the sea is rarely calm. Especially when raising a child with sensory processing disorder, there are storms that can feel endless.

My son's struggles—his intense reactions to sounds or textures—remind me daily that my emotional stability sets the tone for our entire household. By *choosing* calm, I'm not denying the chaos; I'm guiding it toward understanding. This is where Stoic philosophy, with its emphasis on self-mastery, becomes an anchor. My son may need a weighted blanket or noise-canceling headphones to cope, but I, too, need tools—inner ones—to remain steady in the face of his overwhelm.

Having three children means my house is constantly buzzing with needs, interests, and personalities. My son's sensory needs blend with the evolving demands of his siblings, creating a symphony of joy and challenge. Stoicism doesn't pretend to solve every issue overnight—far from it. Instead, it offers a mental framework: cultivate patience, practice empathy, and remember that external events can never fully dictate our inner peace unless we allow them to. I've come to appreciate how these ancient principles are actually a perfect companion to modern parenthood: they remind me to breathe before reacting, to pause and consider how my response will shape my child's sense of safety and belonging.

One thing I've learned through trial and error is that *persistence and repetition* are essential, not just for my children's routines but for my own mindset. Children thrive on structure—I see it in my son's eyes when he knows exactly what comes next. That predictability calms him. But it also calms *me*. Repeated actions, like morning checklists or consistent bedtime rituals, form a secure base for all of us. Yet, there's also a bittersweet truth: *not everything works all the time.* Sometimes the best-laid plans unravel in an instant. The meltdown arrives without warning; the routine we trusted suddenly fails. In these moments, Stoicism reminds me that what truly matters is how I *choose* to respond. Failure isn't a dead end; it's an invitation to refine our methods, remain flexible, and keep going. And on days when the routine *does* click, when the meltdown is avoided and my son beams with pride, it feels like we've touched a small miracle.

My family is my world—my wife, the pillar of our home, and our three children, each with their distinct quirks and gifts. Parenting has given my life a sense of purpose that nothing else could. The laughter of my children, even in the midst of sensory overload or sibling squabbles, is a testament to the resilience of the human spirit. They remind me that love and chaos can coexist. If Stoicism has taught me anything, it's that the smallest victories—a meltdown averted, a new word learned, a shared giggle—can be the building blocks of a life well lived.

No journey is walked alone, and so I extend my heartfelt thanks to you for reading these reflections. By sharing my family's story, I hope to offer a sense of solidarity—whether you're a parent navigating special needs, a guardian striving for patience, or simply someone seeking to live more intentionally. Your presence here means that none of us is alone in this quest to raise empathetic, resilient children. I may not have all the answers, and I suspect you don't either, but together we learn, adapt, and cherish the moments that shine through the clouds.

To me, Stoicism is not about perfect serenity or rigid detachment; it's a daily practice of realigning my thoughts, emotions, and actions with the values I hold dear. Each morning, I recommit to patience—even if it fails me by afternoon. Each evening, I reflect on what went right and what could be adjusted. This ebb and flow is the rhythm of parenthood, a rhythm that shapes both my children's future and my own growth. Thank you for walking this path with me, for sharing in the triumphs and the tribulations, and for believing—like I do—that every day, we can be a little more present, a little more patient, and a little more loving.

day, we can be a little more present, a little more patient, and a little more loving.

www.ingramcontent.com/pod-product-compliance
Lightning Source LLC
Chambersburg PA
CBHW061745070526
44585CB00025B/2811